Europe's Fault Lines

Europe's Fault Lines

Racism and the Rise of the Right

Liz Fekete

VERSO
London • New York

First published by Verso 2018
© Liz Fekete 2018

1 3 5 7 9 10 8 6 4 2

Verso
UK: 6 Meard Street, London W1F 0EG
US: 20 Jay Street, Suite 1010, Brooklyn, NY 11201
versobooks.com

Verso is the imprint of New Left Books

ISBN-13: 978-1-78478-722-6
ISBN-13: 978-1-78478-725-7 (US EBK)
ISBN-13: 978-1-78478-724-0 (UK EBK)

British Library Cataloguing in Publication Data
A catalogue record for this book is available from the British Library

Library of Congress Cataloging-in-Publication Data
A catalog record for this book is available from the Library of Congress

Typeset in Sabon by MJ & N Gavan, Truro, Cornwall
Printed and bound by CPI Group (UK) Ltd, Croydon, CR0 4YY

For Kavita,
daughter, teacher, friend

Contents

Acknowledgements

This book could not have been written without the help of many people, foremost among them A. Sivanandan, my teacher these last thirty-five years, whose political analysis and insights provided the building blocks for everything I have ever written. A massive debt is also owed to both Jenny Bourne and Frances Webber, who read through various drafts and gave of their advice and expertise unstintingly. Chapter 2 builds on an earlier piece written jointly with Frances for *Race & Class*, while an earlier version of material in chapters 3 and 4 was first published in *The Politics of the Right: Socialist Register 2016* (socialistregister.com).

There are many others to thank, including my colleagues Harmit Athwal, Jon Burnett, Anya Edmond and Hazel Waters, as well as Antonia von der Behrens, Arun Kundnani, Mark McGovern, Peter Pelz and Luc Vervaet. I am particularly grateful to Lisa Schäder, who provided brilliant research support on Germany. Finally, I would like to thank Rosie Warren, my commissioning editor at Verso – patient, intellectually incisive, and ever supportive.

Introduction

For some years it has been clear that a coterie of New Right intellectuals in both Europe and North America has been intent on fomenting a reactionary cultural revolution, to shake up and reconfigure politics and take power. *Europe's Fault Lines* sets out to explore the changing dispensation of European politics in turbulent times. On the face of it, the facts after the Brexit referendum, the election of Donald Trump, and the French run-off election that delivered the largest vote to a European far-right presidential candidate since the Second World War have come together in ways that suggest the onward march of the New Right, or even the triumph of fascism. But *Europe's Fault Lines* is not intended to devitalise or scare readers. It may have started out as an interrogation of the burning issues of our time – to discover what is specific about racism, populism and fascism today, and what distinguishes it from the classical fascism of the 1930s; but, in the course of writing, another Europe shone through, one where democratic and anti-fascist traditions are profoundly present.

In an illiberal and more authoritarian state, where the seductive veneer of capitalism has been replaced by its more ugly, brutal and predatory face, there will inevitably be counter-movements against racism and nativism, corporate greed and the social reaction of the right. Though in *Europe's Fault Lines* I foreground the changing nature of state racism at a time of a resurgent right, that does not mean there is no countermelody, no resistance, and no civil disobedience. In fact, this book sets out to remind us that humanitarian, anti-fascist and socialist values are far more deeply rooted in European culture than is authoritarianism.

The Centrality of Resistance

The issues addressed in *Europe's Fault Lines* came to the fore precisely because they were the ones already being taken up by the organisations, human rights defenders, anti-racist activists, campaigning journalists and committed artists that I have been privileged to work with, both as director of the Institute of Race Relations (IRR) and as an advisory editor on *Race & Class*. These people and campaigns challenge, by their very actions, the state and institutional practices that give rise to the various racisms described in the following chapters. Campaigns against Europe's complicity in torture, like those in support of the dual-nationality Ali Aarrass, delivered by the Belgians to the Moroccan torture state, amplify the voices of prisoners and ensure that their sufferings are not erased. The campaigners, mainly women, who founded Joint Enterprise Not Guilty by Association (JENGbA) to fight for a change in UK law have deepened our knowledge of neoliberal incarceration regimes and the war against the poor. States deploy various techniques of duplicity and denial when people die in police stations, prisons or immigration removal centres, or are shot at or tasered on our streets. But the knowledge of how to counter institutional denial through campaigns for truth and justice has been handed down from generation to generation, thanks to organisations like Relatives for Justice (Northern Ireland), United Friends and Families, Inquest (United Kingdom), Collectif Angles Morts (France) and the Oury Jalloh International Independent

Commission (Germany). The Collective Against Islamophobia in France (CCIF), and the many organisations working in the UK to expose the stigmatisation of Muslims via the government's Preventing Violent Extremism agenda (Prevent), knew the taste and feel of anti-Muslim racism long before Islamophobia was theorised in the academy. Issues of institutional racism in policing and state collusion with the far right would not even be on the agenda if it were not for the activities of organisations like the Monitoring Group in London, the Committee on the Administration of Justice in Belfast, NSU-Watch and Reach Out in Germany, and Popular Action Against State Impunity in Spain. Finally, it has been the magnificent efforts of NGOs, independent search-and-rescue missions and humanitarian volunteers who, in the absence of a social state, have taken over its functions – so spotlighting the viciousness of the state's preferred option of abandoning refugees and militarising borders. States have responded by attempting to criminalise their decency. Unbelievably, many Danes, including a former children's ombudsman, have been charged under anti-smuggling laws simply for giving food, clothes, lifts or other forms of help to refugees as they attempted to cross over the bridge from Copenhagen to Malmö, Sweden.

Racism, Neoliberalism and the Market State

The seeds of *Europe's Fault Lines* lie in the previous collection *A Suitable Enemy: Racism, Migration and Islamophobia* (2009), which was based on my work over sixteen years at IRR researching issues of racism and refugee policy in Europe. It was in 1992, just after the anti-migrant pogroms at Hoyerswerda and then Rostock in Germany, that the IRR first began to look at the harmonisation of refugee and immigration policies across Europe, charting the path from the extreme right's call for an exclusive national preference and cultural identity in the 1990s, to the institutionalisation of anti-foreigner racism (xeno-racism) and anti-Muslim principles within European immigration asylum and national security laws in the 2000s. This new book picks up the story from 2009. It examines the accumulated pressures now exposing fundamental fault lines of racism and authoritarianism in Europe. Old racisms may be structured deeply in European thought, but they have been revitalised and spun in new ways under a variety of forces, including that of the War on Terror, the cultural revolution from the right and the migration-linked demonisation of the destitute 'scrounger' (the latter breathing new life, in the process, into social-Darwinist ideas about the 'deviant', 'asocial' and 'workshy'). In the process, xeno-racism, a non-colour-coded and highly malleable form of racism – a way of denigrating and reifying asylum seekers before segregating and/or expelling them, first identified by A. Sivanandan in his 2001 *Race & Class* essay 'Poverty Is the New Black' – has been developed further, with the operation of separate principles for foreigners introduced into the legal and penal systems.

The roots of pre–Second World War authoritarian and illiberal traditions have proved much more intricate and deep than the post-Holocaust Zeitgeist has dared to acknowledge; now reinvigorated, they are bursting out like some sinister and tangled undergrowth. Of course Europe, the continent that gave birth to colonialism, imperialism, scientific racism and eugenics, as well as National Socialism, has a long history of racism and authoritarianism. Understanding this fact, and the continuities it entails with what is happening today, is essential. But 'racism', as A. Sivanandan reminds us, 'never stands still'. It manifests itself in different ways, at different points in time, in terms of 'changes in the economy, the social structure, the system and, above all, the challenges, the resistances, to that system'.

Today, it is the supremacy of the market, as well as war, that is driving changes in society and reshaping the state. An analysis of the 'market state' helps make sense of the various patterns of racism in Europe – as well as the emergence in the United States, a country built on slavery – of an 'America First' movement that has at its heart white nationalism and its political and cultural dominance (backed by the corporate power of tobacco, oil and pharmaceutical companies).

While Europe's support for wars in the Middle East and Arab world have long strengthened enemy images of Muslims and bolstered Islamophobia, the insecurities generated by the globalisation of the world economy and the embrace of neoliberalism have created the climate for nativism ('our own people first'). The classical fascism of the 1930s emerged in a period of imperial rivalries between nation-states. The circumstances today are fundamentally different, as the power of the nation-state, which has become an agent for transnational capital, is much diminished. But it is also true that neo-Nazi and fascist tendencies are springing up in a climate made fertile by the right's embrace of nativism. Holding out the promise of economic protectionism and the end of freedom of movement (in Europe), the nationalists are barely distinguishable from neoliberal globalists when it comes to the privatisation of state assets and the dismembering of the welfare state. Policies of national preference and the politics of fear (of invasion by immigrants, of domination by fanatical Muslims, of the violence of the underclass or the human filth of the global poor) represent the only solution the right holds out to communities fragmented by industrial decline and neoliberal abandonment. Insider–outsider racism, now proactively pursued by the Conservative Party's Brexit state, aims to win over the 'decent working people' to policies that work fundamentally against their interests. Extreme-right electoral parties may pretend they can magic globalisation away, but at some point they come up against the brick wall of economic reality.

Austerity, with its aggressive assault on progressive politics in the field of equalities, labour and civil rights, has accelerated the shift in the social structure. This is no accident. The economics of austerity are a means to an end: any solidarity across race and class threatens a social structure that promotes radical individualism and has been reorganised to meet the demands of the market. Today's European societies are increasingly divided between citizens, demi-citizens and non-citizens, with fundamental rights no longer guaranteed to certain categories of people (defined by race, class, religion, immigration status, incarceration and political beliefs). In this more brutal, less democratic, more atomised, more unequal world, where parliamentary democracies have been hollowed out, new modes of governance emerge which, in co-opting Third Sector actors into market-oriented service delivery, fundamentally undermine civil society. States govern at a distance, outsourcing key responsibilities in the fields of justice and welfare to private companies, with governance increasingly delivered via networks drawn from a nexus of private, state and Third Sector actors.

Increasingly, the fiction of policing by general consent can no longer be maintained. As the state relinquishes many of its functions, and structured violence and social anomie become entrenched in the face of the destruction of the welfare state, technology and biopower allows it to extend its reach into civil society. What we are seeing are police-enforcement-led wars against the *sans papiers*, the multicultural poor, and the black (and increasingly white) disenfranchised. Technology allows for selective repression of dissenting and surplus populations – now subject to what can be termed the control of the surveillance state. Fascism is not just an ideology or a set of ideas – it is an attitude to human life itself. All these developments provide a threat not just to social, civil and democratic rights, but to human dignity.

The perspective I take in this book, then, eschews a boxed-in, academic study of fascism, which almost invariably divorces the study of the far right from a simultaneous study of the state, and the study of fascism itself from popular and state racism. Likewise, in relation to extremism, a metanarrative has been established that leaves the state, or capital, out of any discussion. Central to what follows, therefore, is a discussion of the way in which the neoliberal state across Europe has tried to frame and manage the rise of racism and fascism, by reviving

Cold War anti-totalitarian frameworks (focusing on the twin evils of communism and fascism) that are now woven into the new state counter-extremism and counter-radicalisation programmes that have emerged in the context of the War on Terror.

A Note on Terminology

Europe's Fault Lines is divided into three parts, although certain themes and concepts recur throughout the book. From the outset, readers are introduced to a bewildering array of contemporary anti-immigration, nativist, extreme-right, far-right and neo-Nazi groups. How to categorise such groups – to know, for instance, when to define a tendency as extreme-right, far-right, fascist or a variant of fascist – is a vexed question on which academics, experts, historians and campaigners will inevitably disagree. So here a note about my use of terminology might be useful. I use 'extreme right' to denote those electoral parties that are to the right of traditional conservative parties, especially in terms of their willingness to use racist language and rhetoric. While it may have its roots in pre-war fascist parties, or share some of the traits of a racist, ultra-nationalist or even fascist party, the extreme right tends to work (barely) within constitutional frameworks, incorporating aspects of cultural conservatism and falling short of advocating violence against its opponents. That is what distinguishes the extreme right from the far right, which, with some notable exceptions, does not reject violence and is more clearly associated with a country's ultra-nationalist or fascist past. But it should also be borne in mind that the forming and re-forming of parties and tendencies discussed in *Europe's Fault Lines* are like the movement of the pieces of glass in a kaleidoscope, which take on new patterns and formations with each swivel of the tube. Alternative for Germany, for instance, started out as a Eurosceptic, culturally conservative party, but can now be fairly located within the far-right family. Another term that crops up in the text is 'hard right'. There is now such a crossover between the arguments of nativists, cultural conservatives, nationalists and the extreme right that I decided to use hard right as a way of, first, denoting the new patterns that emerge when various electoral platforms (seemingly discrete) come together and, second, as a means of distinguishing the ideology of the parliamentary hard right from the violent counter-insurgency of the extra-parliamentary ultra-right. But then what must be also borne in mind is the broader political context and wider environment in which ultra-right forces are springing up. We need to question the ways that we have been trained to understand fascism not as the convergence of affinities and affiliations at the periphery and centre of society, but as just another ideology for sale in the 'marketplace of extremisms'. Extreme parties have moved, since the 1990s, from the periphery to the centre of society, consolidating their authority at a local level, and establishing power bases in municipal and regional governments across Europe. The idea of convergences and affinities between the centre and the periphery, and between the extreme right and a newly configured hard right, is a central theme of the book.

As is the concept of collusion. I have been writing about fascism for over thirty years now, and one thing that regularly frustrates me is the way that the threat posed by the extreme and far right is limited to advances at the ballot box. This obscures the fact that states can collude, either directly or indirectly, with the growth of fascism. The policies pursued by the law-and-order arms of the state – police, the military, the security services – are central. Such collusion is most often understood as a clandestine activity framed by the goal of deniability and requiring a culture of impunity, but it can also be the outcome of the instrumental logic of law-enforcement institutions. It should be understood in both the active sense – 'to conspire, connive or collaborate' – and as the failure to act – by 'turning a blind eye' or 'pretended ignorance' of what should 'morally, legally or officially' be opposed. Here, I have learned a great deal from Professor Mark McGovern, an academic expert on collusion,[1] who writes in the context of Northern Ireland – where the British state, acting in the colonial tradition of counter-insurgency, colluded with the crimes of loyalist paramilitary organisations. But McGovern's forensic examination of the nature, pattern and logic of collusion in Northern Ireland and of the links between collusion and a racialised social order has universal application. It is certainly transferable to the policing of the far right in Europe. Collusion can be understood as occurring when state agents (military, intelligence, police) engage with non-state agents in wrongful acts of violence perpetrated by, or linked to, non-state political actors.[2] In today's Europe, a racialised social order, accompanied by a culture that makes 'turning a blind eye' possible, if not desirable, is the context in which collusion occurs, with collusive state practices facilitating the actions of neo-Nazi paramilitaries or terror squads, and confounding investigations into their crimes, including arson, bomb attacks and murder. The concept of collusion, then, gives us a tool to unravel the crimes of the state – vital in a post-Trump world, if we are to protect democracy. The very safety of ethnic, religious and sexual minorities in Europe today depends on the capacity of law enforcement to operate within democratic norms; to resist collusion, whether direct or indirect, with anti-democratic tendencies; and to uphold the rights of minorities, irrespective of whether a Trump or a Le Pen is in power.

I.

The State of Play

1

Preparing for Race War

On 22 July 2011, Anders Behring Breivik killed seventy-seven people in two successive attacks in and around the Norwegian capital. First, he launched a car-bomb attack in the government quarter of central Oslo, killing eight people. Then, dressed in a homemade police uniform, he took a ferry to Oslo's Utøya Island, where he killed a further sixty-nine people, mostly teenagers, attending the Labour Party youth summer camp. At his trial, Breivik described the youngsters he had so cruelly murdered as 'traitors' who had embraced immigration in order to promote an 'Islamic colonisation of Norway'.[1] This was the first major indication of the far right's capacity for mass murder. But since 2011 signs in Europe of an ultra-right grassroots insurgency in the making have been multiplying. And there have been signals, too, of a racist insurrection: arson attacks, petrol bombs, paramilitary and vigilante activities, and the stockpiling of weapons.

Breivik's actions, set against the backdrop of his 1,500-page manifesto *2083: A European Declaration of Independence*, sent out to 1,003 people who he considered fellow-travellers ninety minutes before he embarked on his killing spree, should have alerted people to the dangerous ideological underpinnings of the defence leagues, pro-identity organisations and anti-Islam movements that were mushrooming across Europe. These cheerleaders for ever more wars in the Muslim world (which can broadly be described as counter-jihadism) began to emerge during the 1991 Gulf War, but became more visible and vocal after the events of 11 September 2001.

The lack of official concern over the violent activities of these movements, prior to the Oslo massacre, was not surprising, given the close ideological affinity of counter-jihadism with neoconservatism, militarisation and war, as well as their much-vaunted 'philozionism'.[2]

Another shock was to come in November 2011, this time in the form of revelations about a German neo-Nazi terror cell, the National Socialist Underground (NSU), which had carried out at least ten murders, three bomb attacks and fifteen armed robberies between 1998 and 2007 – acts that could have come straight out of the *Turner Diaries*. It was not just the murder of ten people, mostly of Turkish origin (all executed in the same fashion), that was disturbing, but also the systematic failures and subsequent cover-ups by sixteen regional police forces and intelligence services. Despite the security services having so many paid informers within the neo-Nazi National Democratic Party of Germany (NPD) that they were effectively running it, a white supremacist conspiracy had taken place right under the nose of the security state.

There was more, this time in Greece. On 28 September 2013, the day on which an elite unit within the military had announced it would stage a coup d'état, Nikos Michaloliakos, the leader of Golden Dawn, and four fellow parliamentarians were arrested. Authoritarian dictatorship had only come to an end in the southern European countries of Portugal, Spain and Greece in the mid 1970s. Now, for the first time in four decades, a fascist party had come close to a 'deep-seated and systematic intrusion and infiltration' of the state apparatus in a southern European country.[3] On the same day as the first arrests of Golden Dawn MPs (more were to follow), there was a major purge of the police and military. Investigations were launched into the active involvement of police officers in Golden Dawn, and whether key military camps had been used as training sites for Golden Dawn with the army's connivance. The long list of those subsequently removed, retired or relocated included the head of the Third Counter-Intelligence Division of the National Intelligence Service (who had been responsible for previous investigations into Golden Dawn, and seems to have acted as its chief informant), the chief of the Special Anti-Terrorist Unit and his deputy, the police inspector general for Southern Greece, the chief of the Special Anti-Terrorist Unit, and a police major commanding the DELTA squads (Force of Control Fast Confrontation), which have a history of brutal suppression of left-wing demonstrations.

These extremist actions – and many more, described below – should be understood within the vortex of political change and economic instability that today shapes Europe. Neo-liberalism, austerity and a permanent war culture, failed counter-radicalisation policies, the increasing number of terrorist outrages, the securitisation of migration and the demonisation of refugees have all served to fracture civil society and transform the nature of state power. Extreme-right electoral parties (see Chapter 2) have prospered from insecurity, in turn creating opportunities for the ultra-right. While the more respectable extreme-right electoral parties and the ultra-right street forces do not openly form electoral alliances, their actions clearly complement and encourage each other. Whenever an extreme-right party succeeds in creating a power base, it opens up a space in which an ultra-right violent street culture can flourish.

Racist Mobilisations from Below

It is hard to delineate Europe's ultra-right precisely. It comprises a fluid, constantly mutating, evolving scene. Its various ideological factions are loosely linked in a web of relationships, sometimes splitting off, sometimes coming together in the spaces provided by specific subcultures – around music, football and combat sports, for example. Football firms such as Casuals United, whose members rioted at the Place de la Bourse shrine to the victims of the Brussels terrorist acts of March 2016, are an integral part of the hard right. Hooligans Against Salafists (Ho.Ge.Sa – Hooligans gegen Salafisten), which first emerged in 2014 in Cologne, described itself as a temporary fighting alliance between rival football firms and the 'resistance against the true enemies of the homeland'. For many football firms, like Nice Guys of Djurgården (DFG – Djurgårdens Finna Grabba) and AIK Firman Boys, terrorising 'foreigners' is just another away game. In January 2016, these two football firms rampaged through the streets of Stockholm, handing out leaflets promising to give North African street children 'the punishment they deserve'.

The various factions in the ultra-right include the identitarian movement, strong in France, which has been compared to the so-called alt-right in the United States, the anti-capitalist CasaPound in Italy, and the Autonomous Nationalists, which started in Germany but are now moving both westwards and eastwards. Their long hair and black clothes stand in stark contrast to the appearance of the Free Forces, whose middle-class and professional supporters in Germany are sometimes referred to as the *Kravattennazis* ('Tie Nazis'). Less camouflaged are the white supremacists (Blood and Honour, KKK, Stormfront, White Aryan Resistance), the National Socialists (the most high-profile of which include the National Democratic Party of Germany and the Party of the Danes), the pro-identity movements (such as the Bloc Identitaire and its youth wing Génération Identitaire in France), and defence leagues (such as the notorious English Defence League).

More complex, because more hybrid, are the identity movements among the non-white dispossessed, particularly in France and Belgium, where the anger and sense of persecution among young people from the suburbs have been manipulated

16

by demagogic figures (such as Alain Soral, Dieudonné and Laurent Louis) and directed towards anti-Semitic gesture politics, as epitomised by the giving of the inverted Nazi salute, the 'quenelle'.[4] But it should also be noted that before this current emerged among the marginalised, the ultra-right Jewish Defence League (Ligue de Défense Juive), banned in Israel and the United States but legal in France, was targeting North African and pro-Palestinian gatherings. This fact is seldom noted, as the idea that Jewish nationalism can be racist and violent against Arabs runs against the dominant myth in France of a tolerant 'Judaeo-Christian' homeland, whose harmony is threatened only by Muslim former colonial subjects, who are the sole carriers of anti-Semitism.

Among the more traditional ideological brands on sale in the modern far-right market place are Strasserism (some argue that the Autonomous Nationalists are a continuation of the Strasser brothers' worker-based strand of National Socialism that was rejected by Hitler) and 'third positionism' (anti-capitalist and anti-Marxist), a modernised variation of which can be found in the Italian Fascists of the Third Millennium. Then, of course, there is counter-jihadism, which is best understood as a spectrum with street-fighting forces at one end and cultural conservatives and neoconservative writers at the other. Bringing all of these mutant forms together over specific causes are the nebulous and fanatical fronts that spring up from time to time, seemingly spontaneously, as vehicles for discontent.

Examples of the activities of these fanatical fronts abound – from the summer 2013 protests of so-called 'decent citizens' against 'inadaptable citizens' (namely Roma – see below), which swept through Bohemia in the Czech Republic, to Printemps Français, a homophobic network of Catholic fundamentalists and the far right which, in 2013, brought over 100,000 people out on the streets of Paris against the proposed same-sex marriage law (the largest right-wing demonstration in France for thirty years). More recently, it was Patriotic Europeans Against the Islamisation of the Occident (Patriotische Europäer gegen

17

die Islamisierung des Abendlandes – Pegida) that swept onto the scene, seemingly out of nowhere. Its supporters were dubbed by much of the media, with a nod to the Free Forces, the 'pin-striped Nazis'. Pegida's first march, in Dresden in October 2014, attracted just 200 people. By January 2015, the numbers marching in the streets of Saxony's baroque capital had swelled to an estimated 25,000.

But these are not flash-mobs. Nor are they merely the initiatives of angry white working-class men suffering an excess of alcohol and energy. It would also be wrong to see them as entirely the product of organised fascism, though the fascists act as fixers. They are racist mobilisations from below, swelling up from anger, fear and machismo at the grassroots, and manipulated by the ultra-right, inasmuch as fascism flows from the same springs of racial hatred and social anomie.

From Community Politics ...

They often start out as nebulous, virtual protests on Facebook around some specific local social tension (such as the housing of refugees or Roma, or a planning application for a mosque). From here they are elevated through social media into national causes. So-called 'citizens' initiatives' are organised, uniting the various fascist mutants with so-called 'decent, ordinary citizens' in a frenzy of aggression that is expressed through angry demonstrations in minority neighbourhoods. In the Czech Republic, Roma are referred to in mainstream discourse as the 'inadaptable' – the term used by Himmler in 1942 when he gave the order to deport all remaining Roma and Sinti to Auschwitz because they were 'inadaptable people'.[5] The message is not lost on the far right, which created a Facebook page in June 2013 entitled 'Protest Actions against Inadaptable Citizens', issuing a call to activists to rally in the south Bohemian city of České Budějovice. An estimated 800 neo-Nazis from all over the country travelled to the area in response to the call, and used Molotov cocktails, stones and broken glass to attack a counter-rally of Roma and their supporters on a housing estate on the outskirts of the city. The violence became a weekly occurrence during that whole summer. It was documented in a YouTube film entitled 'Captive Audience', the title borrowing a concept used by Hungarian NGOs in their case against the far-right nationalist paramilitaries (see below). At the European Court it was successfully argued that the purpose of the paramilitaries' incursions into Roma neighbourhoods was to keep the Roma in captivity – preventing them from going to work or to school, trapping them in their homes, and giving them no choice but to listen to racist provocations and threats to kill.

Much is made of the 'ordinariness' of the people who attend the demonstrations of Pegida. But this claim elides the fact that neo-Nazis are considered ordinary in many parts of east Germany. For example, in Dresden, the capital of Saxony, Pegida was born, in a region of the former GDR that was previously very white and monocultural. Research carried out by the University of Bielefeld in 2011 suggested that 45.7 per cent of the population in the Dresden district of Leuben (an NPD stronghold) did not perceive that there was any neo-Nazi problem in their neighbourhood, around a quarter believing that there was no difference between the NPD and other political parties.[6] Though few remember now, it was in Dresden that the Egyptian pharmacist Marwa El Sherbini was murdered in a courtroom, of all places, in July 2009. Marwa, who was three months pregnant, was giving evidence against a neo-Nazi sympathiser who had attacked her in a playground and abused her as an 'Islamist whore' on account of her headscarf. As she was testifying, the defendant rushed across the courtroom and stabbed her eighteen times in the space of thirteen seconds, screaming, 'You have no right to live!' A police officer called to the scene mistook El Sherbini's husband, Elwi Ali Okaz, who was wrestling with the killer, for the assailant, and shot him, causing him serious injuries, though he survived. An attempt by Dr Sabine Schiffer, director of the Institute for Media Responsibility, to raise further questions about the killing, and to ask whether media portrayals of Muslims might have influenced the police officer who shot El Sherbini's husband, resulted in Schiffer's prosecution for slandering a police officer.

Marwa El Sherbini's murder should have led to a sustained investigation of the culture of fascism that had developed unchecked at the community level, influenced by the NPD and the Free Forces. This did not happen. The fact that the NPD had a total of seventy-seven elected representatives in the state of Saxony at the time of El Sherbini's murder could have served as the first warning of deep underlying problems. But it did not – and nor did subsequent revelations about the NSU. This neo-Nazi terror cell, headed by two men and one woman, executed ten people, nine from a migrant background, between 2000 and 2007. Most probably inspired by Blood and Honour, Combat 18 and the organisational concept of leaderless resistance, they never claimed responsibility for their crimes, which only became public after a horrific DVD celebrating the murders was sent out to media outlets days after the NSU's Uwe Böhnhardt and Uwe Mundlos set their getaway car on fire, killing themselves, following a botched armed robbery and police chase in Eisenach, Thuringia. It was in Saxony, in the town of Zwickau, close to the Czech border, that the NSU trio Böhnhardt, Mundlos and Beate Zschäpe (who sent the DVD to the press) first went underground, having been forced to take to the road after a bomb-making factory was found in a garage the group was renting in Jena, Thuringia, in 1998. Murder after murder took place, yet the perpetrators were never found. The same gun was used in nine of the murders, but the police were too busy investigating and defaming the victims' families to connect the dots.

Although the official German narrative about the NSU case maintains otherwise, the NSU was not a cell, but a complex including a number of actors, such as the neo-Nazi Blood and Honour network, which helped the NSU stay under the radar for over a decade by providing safe houses, passports, medical aid and weapons. This much has been established incontrovertibly by the campaigning group NSU-Watch, which has been monitoring the trial of Beate Zschäpe, the NSU's supposedly sole surviving member, and four accessories since it started in Munich in May 2013. But the international coverage of the rise of Pegida is removed from the context of this history, as though the 'pinstriped Nazis' came from nowhere.

A close examination of its programme and activities at that time shows that, for Pegida, Islam serves merely as a convenient code-word; its anti-Islam agenda, as Anthony Fano Fernadez has pointed out, is an act of 'sly, tactical opportunism'.[7] Pegida is a classic far-right anti-immigration movement. Throughout 2013–14 in Saxony, there were 'citizens' initiatives' against refugees, with protests outside asylum reception centres in towns such as Chemnitz and Schneeberg in the Ore mountains, and Borna near Leipzig. Pegida's supporters want to keep this part of east Germany white and free from immigrants. They are particularly angry that the federal government is dispersing asylum seekers from Syria to the region, and want to force it to reverse this policy. Pegida issued a six-point list of demands, one of which was a call for more 'direct democracy' (a local referendum to keep out refugees). In the meantime, since Pegida's emergence (and irrespective of its subsequent splits, outlined below), fascist mobilisations and racist violence against refugees have sky-rocketed across Germany, particularly in Saxony-Anhalt and Bavaria. Reporters Without Borders also noted increasing attacks on journalists in the context of Pegida's use of the slogan, 'Lying press, shut up!', which has clear Nazi connotations. Markus Nierth, the mayor of Tröglitz, resigned, citing concerns for his family's safety, after the NPD announced that the latest of a series of rallies, opposing a modest proposal by the town council to host fifty refugees, would end outside his home. Meanwhile, the mayor of Magdeburg, where the sister organisation Magida was launched, was offered police protection after receiving death threats, leading a Green Party member of the regional parliament, Sebastian Striegel, to tweet in early 2015: 'It is cold here: smear campaigns against refugees, death

21

threats against politicians, mayors resigning out of fear for their families.'

Worse was to come. The situation deteriorated still further throughout 2015–16. As 'citizens' initiatives' formed against the dispersal of Syrian refugees, there was a fivefold increase in attacks on refugee accommodation, with around ten anti-migrant attacks a day, and yet more vicious attacks on refugee-friendly politicians, demonised as traitors.

These events included the attempted murder of Henriette Reker, stabbed in the neck in October 2015, on the day before she was elected mayor of Cologne, by a fascist sympathiser who targeted her because of her pro-refugee views, and the attack in September 2016 on Joachim Kebschull, the refugee-supporting sixty-one-year-old mayor of the small German northern town of Oersdorf, who was left unconscious after being struck with a blunt instrument.

But at the same time, an alarming diversification was taking place in the demographic makeup of the perpetrators of violence, with xenophobic attacks becoming the 'new normal'. Anti-racist organisations suggest that the majority of attacks on refugee accommodation were carried out and organised not by the far right, but by freelance xenophobes whose latent far-right sympathies, previously inhibited, were now released. The police routinely downplayed the violence, justifying a lack of arrests by citing the wider silence surrounding such crimes: no witnesses, no suspects, no evidence. The fivefold increase in levels of racist violence in the UK in the immediate aftermath of the referendum on EU membership in July 2016, and the failure to find the culprits, bears comparison with Germany, as those with strong xenophobic attitudes felt vindicated by the referendum result (which was perceived to be a vote against immigration) and engaged in what has been described as 'celebratory racism'.[8] In the UK, the violence, which was both verbal and physical, was fairly evenly spread across the country, from towns and cities to leafy suburbs, while in Germany it was rural communities, predominantly in the east, that saw the greatest upsurge. As refugee accommodation targeted for arson was most often uninhabited (the refugees had not arrived), such 'victimless crime' was tacitly backed by villagers who had strongly opposed the refugee centres in the first place. As Ben Mauk explains, 'To classify arson as the exclusive work of gangs and fanatics is to underestimate its appeal as a weapon of the underclass. The invention of arson belongs in the village.'[9]

... to Criminality and Paramilitarism

Nevertheless, when it comes to attacks on symbolic locations – mosques, refugee centres, migrant camps or left-wing targets – involving guns, hand grenades, petrol and nail bombs, the most likely culprits are still to be found within the ultra-right, which, though it may consist of various strands, has a shared affinity for criminality. Today's ultra-right scene offers apprenticeships in pimping and extortion, money laundering, drug- and arms-running, human smuggling, vigilantism and armed combat (Scandinavian neo-Nazis are among those fighting in Ukraine). In Saxony, there are so many unsolved ultra-right criminal acts against refugees that anti-fascists now speak of 'the new NSU', a reference to the phenomenon of attacks on asylum centres and the state's failure to protect them. Major trials involving ultra-right criminal conspiracies have either taken place in recent years or are ongoing in many countries, including Germany (NSU, White Wolves Terror Crew, Old School Society, Freital Group),[10] Spain (Anti-System Front), Austria (Objekt 21), Italy (New Order), France (White Wolves Klan) and Hungary (Roma serial murders by neo-Nazis who formed their own private militia). All reveal collusion, either direct or indirect, between the neo-Nazis, the police, the military, the intelligence services, or a mixture of these elements. In 2016, in Greece, the trial continues of seventy-two members of Golden Dawn (including eighteen MPs) on charges of forming a criminal organisation, weapons procurement, soliciting the murder of the anti-fascist rapper Pavlos Fysass in Athens, the attempted murder of three Egyptian fishermen in Perama, near Piraeus, and the near-fatal attack on the president of the metalworkers' union and other Communist trades unionists in the dockyards of Piraeus. In June 2013, Clément Méric, an eighteen-year-old French activist from the Parti de Gauche, was left brain-dead after being punched in the face by a skinhead wearing a knuckle-duster during a fight between left-wingers and skinheads near a railway station in the 9th district of Paris. The trial for manslaughter of three of the skinheads linked to Troisième Voie (Third Way), a private militia that has since been banned, has yet to take place. Since then, many more have died in far-right-inspired attacks. In Finland, Jimi Karttunen, a twenty-eight-year-old anti-racist, died of head injuries sustained during an attack at Helsinki railway station by a member of the Finnish Resistance Movement. Karttunen's assailant was eventually cleared of aggravated assault, receiving a two-year sentence for grievous bodily harm. The murder of the UK Labour Party MP Joanne Cox took place in June 2016 in the small market town of Birstall, West Yorkshire, in the run-up to the EU referendum. Five months later, Thomas Mair, a white supremacist who repeatedly shouted, 'Britain First!' as he shot and stabbed the MP, was convicted for her murder.

Such blatant political killings are bad enough, but there is also evidence of ultra-right elements infiltrating the forces of 'law and order' so as to compound or confound the issue. One would have thought that, in Germany at least, the circumstances surrounding the shooting dead in Bavaria of a police officer by the leader of Citizens of the Reich would have made police affiliation to far-right groups a cause for immediate action. It seems possible that the armed far-right leader may have been tipped off about an imminent raid on his home to confiscate weapons. Fifteen police officers are now suspected of association with Citizens of the Reich, including two who were part of a WhatsApp group that had previously chatted with the killer. After the arrest in May 2017 of a first lieutenant in the German army (he had, it is alleged, created a false identity as a Syrian refugee in order to mount a terror attack), the authorities announced the possibility that a neo-Nazi cell of at least five people might exist within the army.

Privatised far-right security is another concern. In the eastern German state of Saxony – where, as we have seen, ultra-right assaults on refugee centres are numerous – the neo-Nazi NPD has openly called on supporters to join Saxony's Security Watch – a volunteer civilian unit that supports the police – arguing that membership would provide an opportunity for its activists to work completely legally in a security-related field. According to Popular Action Against Impunity, the situation in north-east Spain following the collapse of the trial of eighteen members of the Anti-System Front (FAS) in Autumn 2014 also raises issues of collusion between the neo-Nazis and the military, as well as rogue police officers who allegedly tipped off FAS about an ongoing police investigation. As a coalition of left political groups and social organisations, Popular Action Against Impunity is affected by the neo-Nazi violence in north-east Spain, which has included bomb attacks against left-wing and trades-union targets, mosques, social centres and official ceremonies and public events (more than twenty bomb attacks between 2005 and 2008 remain unsolved by the police). At the trial of the FAS members, two of whom were from the military and one the son of a police officer, the judge ruled police intercept evidence inadmissible on the grounds that phone taps should not have been authorised, since hawking arms online was a normal activity. Among the weapons seized during the police raids that preceded the trial was a grenade launcher.

The ultra-right has also taken it upon itself to impose its own law – namely, vigilante justice – with its own private militias and paramilitary squads. In Greece, prior to the arrest of the organisation's MPs, black-clad Golden Dawn supporters armed with clubs were in the habit of sweeping through migrant areas on motorbikes, beating everyone in sight. Its use of battalion squads of paramilitary fighters to police and intimidate certain neighbourhoods all took place under the watchful eye of the Hellenic Police. Between August 2012 and February 2013, the Hellenic Police were involved in their own sweep against migrants, in the form of the racial profiling exercise Operation Xenios Zeus. This led to almost 85,000 suspected foreigners being forcibly taken to a police station for verification of their immigration status (94 per cent were found to have a legal right to remain in Greece). At the trial of Golden Dawn, reported on every day by the websites Golden Dawn Watch and Jail Golden Dawn since it began in April 2015, compelling evidence has emerged to suggest that, from 2010 to 2013, Golden Dawn operated as a para-state agency, cleansing neighbourhoods with the collusion of local police – and that it financed its activities through protection rackets, blackmailing shop-owners, selling weaponry used by its battalion squads, and providing services to businessmen. Collusion also extended to the National Intelligence Service (EYP), one high-ranking official responsible for the telephone surveillance of Golden Dawn resigning in 2013 after media allegations of his links to the organisation.

Such vigilantism and paramilitarism show no signs of abating. No country or region of Europe is immune, with so-called civilian militias attempting to create a climate of low-intensity terror in contested areas, and emerging in areas where the far right already has a base. The Roma, living in shacks and sheds in the poor villages of north-eastern Hungary, were the first targets of the black-clad militia of the Civic Guard Association for a Better Future (a revival of the Second World War fascist militia, the Arrow Cross) and the neo-Nazi Outlaw Army. The latter organisation has routinely patrolled Roma neighbourhoods armed with whips and axes, singing war songs, bellowing abuse, shining floodlights into the windows of Roma families at night and carrying out random inspections of yards and living accommodation 'for cleanliness'. But since Viktor Orbán's militarisation of the Hungarian border, the likes of the 'field guards' of the Jobbik mayor of Ásotthalom (a village on the Hungarian–Serbian border) have been encouraged. The situation in Bulgaria, where the Bulgarian National Front Shipka (a reference to a battle in 1887 in which a Russo-Bulgarian force defeated the Ottoman Turks) patrols the Bulgarian–Turkish border dressed in military fatigues, is equally alarming. Official support (even adulation) for the Organisation for the Protection of Bulgarian Citizens, and freelancers like the twenty-nine-year-old semi-professional wrestler Dinko Valev, was only withdrawn after the international media broadcast a graphic video showing armed civilians tying up refugees, forcing them to lie down and shouting, 'No Bulgaria! Go Back to Turkey!'

Nor are the countries of northern and western Europe immune from the emergence of vigilante militias, including anti-Islamic groups. In France, much vigilante activity in Calais seems to take place under the radar. In 2016 the Bar Human Rights Committee of England and Wales (BHRC) carried out a fact-finding mission to the unofficial makeshift 'Jungle' camp in Calais (completely demolished in October of that year).[11] The report drew attention not only to worrying levels of violence inside the camp, but also to generalised and specific violence emanating from the police. It is the possibility that members of the CRS riot squad, accused of beating camp residents with batons, sticks and truncheons, could be colluding either directly or indirectly with vigilante groups that is of most concern, given that the CRS has traditionally been linked to high levels of support for the extreme right. A far-right anti-migrant group, Sauvons Calais, had also been active in Calais since 2013, justifying its marches and provocations on the grounds that the town's mayor, Natacha Bouchert, had called on citizens to inform on migrants squatting in the town. Police have been accused of failing to take action, as far-right groups, now including Génération Identitaire, travel to Calais with the specific intention of targeting migrants. BHRC was concerned that many of the Jungle camp's residents it interviewed spoke of the police as possibly complicit in vigilantism, claiming that attackers often wore police uniform, or had similar batons or boots to the CRS.

Vigilante patrols, both at borders and internally, often take on an anti-Islamic character, acting to stop the 'Muslim invasion'. In 2014, Britain First, an offshoot of the British National Party whose structures are inspired by Ulster loyalism in Northern Ireland, organised a series of Christian patrols and invasions of mosques, all in the name of protecting British and Christian morality. Such activities came to a temporary halt in 2017, when the High Court served an injunction on its leaders banning them from mosques across England and Wales for the next three years. The latest pan-European development comes in the form of the Soldiers of Odin, which first emerged in the northern Finnish border town of Kemi, before expanding into the Nordic and Baltic countries, then the Dutch towns of Groningen and Winschoten, and even popping up in Ireland. Claiming to defend native women against 'Islamist intruders', they unite around slogans such as 'Loyalty, respect, honour!', assuming police functions and carrying out patrols.

Superficially, it may seem that these civilian militias and vigilante squads are free agents, operating without the official endorsement of the state; but there is much in the relationship between states and ultra-right vigilantism that makes the dividing line ambiguous. In eastern Europe, civilian militias are either silently tolerated or actively encouraged – particularly by elected officials from extreme-right parties. We saw this in the case of Hungary, where the armed 'field guards' of the extreme-right Jobbik mayor of Ásotthalom are part of the local framework of institutional authority. It is the electoral extreme right, with its local power bases – now very much part of that mainstream political culture – that is emboldening the ultra-right across Europe. Now firmly established in European national and local governments, the extreme right's ability to determine electoral outcomes has shaken the political centre to its core – but only because mainstream political parties have acted as facilitators. By, on the one hand, implementing nativist and anti-Muslim policies and laws, and, on the other, scapegoating refugees, Muslims, Roma and the 'indolent poor' as the 'shirkers' who hold the 'strivers' back, mainstream politicians amplify the perspectives of extreme-right and anti-immigration movements. Such movements advance by pushing at the boundaries of respectable discourse, and operating surreptitiously just within constitutional frameworks, falling just short of advocating physical violence against those who oppose their policies.

2

Understanding the Extreme Right

Back in the late 1980s, the extreme right was just emerging as a viable electoral force, and some of the anti-immigration, anti-Islam parties now breaking the mould of European politics had yet to be established. The first parliamentary incursions of this motley crew of xenophobic populists were rebuffed by the other parties, along with the extreme right's policies of exclusive national preference. European politicians had favoured the isolation tactics of the so-called 'cordon sanitaire' approach to fascism since 1945. Such an approach allowed politicians to establish their anti-fascist credentials while ignoring the reasons for the extreme right's electoral appeal. Fascism was defined as a problem at the margins of society, a kind of gangrenous limb that needed to be cut off to preserve the health of the body politic. Many academic studies of fascism also let mainstream politics off the hook by suggesting that it was the presence of the extreme right that pushed the political centre of gravity rightwards – for instance, on issues of immigration and asylum. This conveniently ignored the affinities between the extreme right and the centre, and the convergence of interests around a whole host of issues that has arisen since the early 1990s, as laid out below.

The first convergence – over refugees – came as a result of the collapse of the Soviet Union, the break-up of the former

Yugoslavia, and the movement of refugees from authoritarian states in the Global South that were backed by Western powers and subjected to structural adjustment programmes – such as Sri Lanka, Zimbabwe, Nigeria, Zaire/DRC, Algeria and Uganda. Globalisation, more than the extreme right, was driving the securitisation of asylum and immigration policies. The convergence of extreme-right anti-refugee racism with the EU's need to abandon a humanitarian approach to asylum and militarise its borders was first seen in the early 1990s, after the neo-Nazi pogroms in 1991 in Hoyerswerda, Saxony, and in 1992 in the eastern coastal city of Rostock. When migrant contract workers and refugees were attacked on the streets, driven out of their hostels by firebombs, Chancellor Kohl effectively rewarded the neo-Nazis by abandoning Article 16 of the German Constitution, which guaranteed the right to asylum. From here on, asylum policy was harmonised at an EU level, land and sea borders were militarised, and a special prison regime was introduced for asylum seekers – described by the Italian philosopher Giorgio Agamben as a reconfiguration of the concentration camps first used by the Spanish in Cuba and the British for Afrikaner prisoners during the Boer War.

Convergence on asylum was followed by convergence on employment and social rights for migrants, in the context of the retrenchment of the welfare state. In the early 1990s, nativism – the policy of protecting the interests of native-born or established inhabitants against those of immigrants – had been associated with the extreme right. No longer. Today, it is far harder for migrants to obtain residence rights, and nativism is the norm in employment law, in addition to providing the rationale for access to the welfare state. There has been a convergence between the extreme right's xenophobia and the mainstream political parties' broad support for the rationing of welfare provision to exclude 'foreigners'. Even the anti-EU positions of the extreme right converge with the views of protectionists within centre-right nationalist camps, making it much more difficult to distinguish between centre-right and extreme-right branches of Euroscepticism. The right per se sings today from the same nativist hymn sheet, the melody also being taken up by the centre left, which has done much to accommodate to the new status quo. One of the most crass examples of this centre-left adoption of rightist themes was provided by New Labour which, as part of its campaign to win the 2015 general election, approved the distribution of a 'controls on immigration' mug – available for sale from the party's online outlet.

The third strong current – this time emanating from the War on Terror – has also led to convergences across the political spectrum on cultural policies towards minority communities. This recalibration of mainstream politics has considerably emboldened the extreme right, vindicating as it does its carefully crafted anti-multiculturalist narrative. The older, established extreme-right parties, like the Alleanza Nazionale (subsequently incorporated into Italy's People of Freedom Alliance), the Front National in France and the Freedom Party in Austria have roots in a fascist past. But that they survived in the post-war period (and went on to prosper from the late 1990s onwards) owes much to a coterie of New Right intellectuals who established think tanks and journals, patiently infiltrating the media and the education system. It was the New Right, particularly in France and the UK, that shifted the mainstream debate from 'race' towards 'culture' and 'ethnicity', coding their arguments in terms of ethnic difference and the threat posed to national identity and values by cultures that do not mix (see Chapter 3).

But in the mid 1990s, the New Right was forced to retreat somewhat. Internationally, the end of apartheid in 1994 and the iconic status afforded to Nelson Mandela made their arguments, including the defence of separate development on the grounds that different cultures do not mix, unfashionable. And within EU countries the aspirations of second- and third-generation immigrants who were 'here to stay, here to fight' meant that even the most intransigent governments had to acknowledge realities, reform citizenship laws and loosen the grip of discrimination (Germany did not recognise it was a country of immigration until 2005, preferring to sustain the apparatus of a 'guestworker' system). But the Al-Qaeda attacks on the World Trade Center and the Pentagon in the United States on 11 September 2001 were to bring to an end any tentative steps towards a fuller acknowledgement of multicultural realities.

The European nations gathered together in an international coalition of the willing to invade Afghanistan and Iraq, and the subsequent war mentality provided a massive boost to the extreme right, with a new round of convergences between it and the centre. The fact that European policies on integration were recalibrated, and a new yardstick for measuring integration was introduced – no longer judged so much on social and economic terms (based on access to the labour market, educational achievement and so on) but around the nebulous concept of 'values' – served as Viagra to the ideologues of the New Right, as in Samuel Huntington's infamous 'clash of civilizations' thesis. By 2011, anti-multiculturalism was no longer the preserve of New Right intellectuals, or maverick writers like Thilo Sarrazin whose polemic *Deutschland Shafft Sich Ab* ('Germany Abolishes Itself') became an overnight bestseller (its central argument was that multiculturalism and Muslims of poor genetic stock were to blame for failures in integration). An influential section within the liberal literati, divorced from social justice struggles but powerful in debates around censorship and freedom of speech, were soon supporting illiberal state policies towards minorities, in what will surely be seen retrospectively as a *trahison des clercs*.

Leaders of the conservative right across Europe publicly attacked what David Cameron, in a strategic intervention in Munich, called the 'state doctrine of multiculturalism'. Since then all governments in Europe – even the Netherlands and Sweden, which, like the UK, were traditionally more open to cultural pluralism – have introduced assimilationist and 'colour-blind' policies, constantly upbraiding cultural and religious minorities for their failure to adopt the 'values' of the dominant culture. This, of course, proved grist to the mill of the advancing army of the extreme right, right-wing populists and demagogues, which today comprise the second- or third-most powerful parliamentary political force in countries as diverse as Germany, Hungary, Norway, France, Denmark, Italy, Finland, the Netherlands and Sweden. It has also emboldened the cultural conservative and New Right intelligentsia. Once again in the ascendancy, these commentators act as a bridge between parliamentarianism and militancy, giving intellectual respectability to hard-right ideas through such journals as, in France, *Causeur*, *Minute* and *Valeurs Actuelles*; in Germany, *Compact*; in Austria, *Info-DIRECT*; in Italy, *L'Occidentale* and *Fare Quadrato*; and in the UK, the *Spectator*.

The Extreme Right in Power

The electoral popularity of the extreme right brought with it access to generous amounts of state funding, both from national coffers and the European parliament. This in turn allowed for consolidation at the local level, the extreme right establishing power-bases in municipal and regional governments across Europe. In France, FN-backed mayors now control twelve municipalities (in the northern 'rust belt' and in southern France, where poverty is held at bay by tourism). In Hungary, the anti-Semitic and anti-Roma mayors of Jobbik rule the Magyar roost in twenty municipalities, mostly in rural villages where the Roma live in absolute poverty. Meanwhile, Skåne in southern Sweden has long been a bastion of the far-right Sweden Democrats; The Hague, and the municipality of Almere in the province of Flevoland, have been strongholds for the maverick Dutch demagogue Geert Wilders, who in 2017 expanded his base to Rotterdam; and Veneto has long been a fortress of Italy's Northern League. Extreme-right penetration of local and regional government has led to clusters of extreme-right support developing in neighbouring electoral zones, particularly in former industrial heartlands and depopulated rural areas. The latest development in this cumulative phenomenon is the rapid rise of Alternative for Germany, which has now broken through the historic East/West divide to establish a presence for itself in thirteen out of Germany's sixteen state parliaments.

But this is no linear march from the margins to the centre; nor is it a story of seizing victory via the parliamentary road to power. The authoritarian personality and the cult of charismatic (usually macho) leadership do not lend themselves to internal stability. Hence, extreme-right political parties are even more prone to in-fighting than other political groupings – witness the plummeting electoral fortunes of the United Kingdom Independence Party (UKIP), since its leader Nigel Farage and financier Arron Banks left for pastures new. Geert Wilders has fixed the constitutional make-up of the PvV to his advantage. The organisation is not registered as a political party but as an association, which means it does not receive state subsidies and does not have to declare its donors. It has no membership (other than Wilders himself) and no local branches, and exists solely to promote Geert Wilders.

Once ensconced in town halls, extreme-right and anti-immigrant parties also begin to look as jaded and as self-serving as the traditional elites they routinely denounce. A corruption scandal erupted in 2008 soon after the death in a car crash of the Austrian extreme-right leader Jörg Haider. He had received kickbacks during the privatisation of state-owned companies and cash injections running into millions of dollars from Saddam Hussein and Colonel Gaddafi, and was further linked to money laundering, the establishment of offshore banks and the near bankruptcy of the regional bank. It was this crony capitalism that lost the extreme right the state premiership of Carinthia, which Haider had governed from 1999 to 2008. More recently, Gianni Alemmano, the 'post-fascist' mayor of Rome from 2008 to 2013, was arrested as part of the Cupola

Romana (Mafia Capitale) investigation into corrupt links between City Hall officials, neo-fascist militias and a criminal mafia, with the town hall under Alemmano's control outsourcing the running of social services (including accommodation centres for migrants and Roma) to an organisation linked to a fascist mafia boss.[1]

The FN won its twelve mayoralties in France in 2014 on the back of promises that it would be different from career-driven, elitist politicians. But it did not take FN mayors long to break their pre-election pledges not to accept an accumulation of mandates (*cumul des mandates*, the practice of having two or more elective offices at different levels of government). More than a score of FN candidates in the March 2015 local elections were over ninety years old, including a 100-year-old woman living in sheltered accommodation. At the moment, the FN's political programme, despite its promises of a protectionist economic policy, largely consists of promoting culture wars, the latest being over the burkini on southern Mediterranean beaches. But while its anti-Muslim policies reflect the racism of the centre, it is deliberately attempting to test the boundaries of legality, by illegally collecting data on the number and names of all Muslim children in local schools in Beziers, organising referendums to stop the dispersal of refugees following the breakup of the 'Jungle' at Calais, and ratcheting up the debate about the death penalty. Since securing its twelve mayoralties, the FN has focused on education (banning halal meat in the school canteen); environment and planning law (blocking applications to open up mosques, Islamic schools and kebab shops); cultural policy ('Pork Fests', removal of 'cosmopolitan' public artworks, cancellation of festivals with progressive content such as celebrating the abolition of slavery, renaming of streets); public order (curfews for young people in socially deprived areas, bylaws stopping the hanging out of washing and the beating of rugs between certain hours).

Once again, this is a strategy that owes much to the Islamophobia of Europe's centre: the extreme right's patriot games and culture wars reflect the political centre's embrace of laws specifically aimed at driving out all visible traces of Islam from public life in Europe. In its war against Muslims, the extreme right elsewhere takes inspiration from France, the first country to ban school students and civil servants from wearing the hijab, and then to ban the wearing of full-face veils in any public place. And it takes inspiration also from Switzerland, which, following a 2009 referendum masterminded by the right-wing populist Swiss People's Party (SVP), became the first European country to ban the construction of minarets on mosques.[2]

Convergence on Crime and Punishment

But despite the extreme right's limited approach to governance, one should be alert to the dangers of a new convergence between the extreme right and the politics of the centre – an affinity that is already delivering fresh sources of power to the ultra-right that go well beyond 'the street'. This is a convergence that exceeds the terrains of culture, religion and minority policies, too, and is now being played out on the battlefield of crime and punishment. And it is all part of a broader convergence that is not just one between the ideologies of political parties, but between transnational capital, the military–security–industrial complex, media barons and the powerful law-and-order lobbies.[3] Transnational policing forums have served as meeting points for all those who want to expand the arsenal of police weaponry, further militarise urban spaces, and loosen inhibitions about the use of torture, shoot-to-kill policies and the return of the death penalty (a universal demand of Europe's extreme right). Already, the continent of Enlightenment values is one that practises torture – not by getting its hands dirty, of course, but by outsourcing the physical act to coalition partners in the War on Terror. Even before the 2016 terrorist outrages in Belgium, France and Germany, the January 2015 Charlie Hebdo and kosher grocery store massacres in Paris, the shoot-out in Verviers, Belgium, and the gun attacks in Copenhagen furnished justifications for the militarisation of the streets on a scale unprecedented in the post-colonial period. Simultaneously, the introduction of austerity has led to an exponential attack on social rights, human rights and democratic standards. The space for individual rights and freedoms is rapidly shrinking.

We need to pay attention to various signs. In an expanded security state, and in an era where policing and even war are being privatised, the ultra-right is among those moving into an expanded market for security – a market that relies on outsourcing. In Germany, where there are now nearly as many private security guards as police officers, neo-Nazis have attempted to find a niche within an outsourced, deregulated market. According to a secret service estimate, one in ten neo-Nazis known to the intelligence services in the state of Brandenburg is employed in the private security industry. Back in 2013, a contractor at an Amazon warehouse was exposed for having employed the subcontractor Hensel European Security Services (its initials alluding to Rudolf Hess) to ensure work discipline among its mostly migrant workforce. Crucially, with the increased privatisation of asylum care, neo-Nazi security guards now have direct access and authority over refugees. As Priska Komaromi puts it, 'would-be attackers' are quite literally being given 'the keys to their victims' doors'.[4] Komaromi presents a number of case-studies in her research, many involving neo-Nazi security guards, but others linked to a wider culture of racism within the security sector. In one case from North Rhine-Westphalia, security guards subcontracted by the firm SKI, which in turn had been subcontracted to provide security by European Homecare (one of the biggest private companies running asylum centres in Germany), were filmed subjecting asylum seekers to Guantánamo-style violence and abuse. Another case involved the Dresden contractor, Ihre Wache GmbH, which local newspapers reported was hiring neo-Nazis. Yet another scandal came to light in February 2015, in the rural town of

Clausnitz, Saxony. A mob blocked a bus full of refugees heading to a refugee centre, the director of which, it turned out, was an active member of Alternative for Germany (AfD). To add insult to injury, his brother, it later emerged, played a leading role in organising the mob. Another company, PeWoBe, lost its contract to run nine hostels for asylum seekers in Berlin after emails written by company managers mocking refugee children and joking about disposing of their bodies 'in a large-volume crematorium', were leaked to the *Bild* newspaper. Earlier, in December 2015, security guards were replaced at another Berlin reception centre after they were caught chanting neo-Nazi slogans as they attempted to keep order.

Far-right voting patterns among law-enforcement and security officers are another sign of the law-and-order convergence, as is the increasing use of disproportionate force by police in everyday encounters, leading to more deaths of black people, Muslims, Roma and migrants in the custody of the police.[5] In Belgium, Hungary and France, police officers have not been shy about putting themselves forward as candidates on an extreme-right electoral list: notably Judit Szima, the secretary general of a Hungarian police trades union who stood as the Jobbik candidate in the 2009 European parliamentary elections; a number of CRS police officers, including Jean-Louis Chabaille, a commander in the Île-de-France CRS, who were on the 2012 FN election list; and, in Belgium, two former police commissioners in Brussels and Antwerp.[6] In addition, Hendrik Rottmann, who works for German military intelligence, is a councillor in Cologne for AfD. While studies of police voting patterns are few and far between, they do suggest strong support for extreme- and even far-right parties. In Greece, in 2012, the *To Vima* newspaper looked at election results in Athens constituencies located close to police stations, concluding on the basis of its sample that more than half of all police officers in Greece had voted for Golden Dawn in the general election. An analysis conducted by the French CNRS research centre at the end of 2015 concluded that a notable increase in FN support derived from the police and the military, 51.5 per cent of whom said they would vote for the FN, compared to only 30 per cent in 2012. And on the eve of the French presidential election in 2017, the Ifop polling firm released statistics indicating that, while 51 per cent of the gendarmeries were set to vote for Le Pen, among the mobile gendarmeries, which play a frontline role in policing disturbances, the figure was more like 65 per cent. The militarisation of the streets and public order policing (as represented by the transnational 'pop-up armies' assembled at G8 summits),[7] and the attack on the rights to protest and to freedom of assembly are further omens of dangers ahead. We have already seen, at the Genoa Summit in 2001, an out-of-control, fascist-style Italian riot squad launching a brutal assault on peaceful protestors, before illegally detaining and torturing them.[8] The pattern was repeated at the Attica General Police Directorate (GADA) in September 2012, when Greek anti-fascists were beaten, forced to strip naked and kept awake all night, with torches and lasers shone in their eyes by police officers, some of whom threatened to hand their details over to Golden Dawn.[9] The Spanish Law for the Protection and Security of Citizens (dubbed the 'citizens' repression bill') has introduced new crimes of obstructing authority (police officers can issue on-the-spot fines against those who show a 'lack of respect'), and provides for fines of up to €600,000 for anyone who causes 'insults or outrages to Spain, the autonomous communities, institutions, symbols, anthems or emblems'.[10]

Divergence on Globalisation

There is one area, though, where a chasm has opened up between the neoliberal centre and the extreme right, and between the extreme and ultra-right, and that is over globalisation. The fact that the extreme right stands for economic autarky and a strong state inevitably brings it into conflict with a market state in hock to transnational capital (although, notably, the pure counter-jihadi strain of fascism does not oppose globalisation but embraces it inasmuch as it associates it with US hegemony, state militarisation and the transnational military–industrial–security complex). The relationship between the traditional European extreme right and national capital is somewhat complex. Although on the surface the extremists appear to stand simply for national economic protectionism, there is a suspicion that they also work behind the scenes to form an alternative transnational pole to globalisation – a new international brotherhood of nation-states. The election of Donald Trump as the forty-fifth president of the United States will certainly have emboldened them, though it is by no means clear at the moment whether his election will ultimately play out in their favour, in Europe at least.

It is significant that, despite its anti-globalisation message and its promise of 'economic patriotism', the extreme right has formulated no radical critique of transnational capital, and has no economic or employment programmes beyond more nativism and more workfare for 'social delinquents' and 'scroungers'. In public declarations, the extreme right describes globalisation primarily in terms of cultural imperialism. Globalisation is synonymous with liberalism, cosmopolitanism, and with the US, European and transnational liberal elites who impose multiculturalism, feminism, gay marriage and transgender rights upon national cultures, which become diluted as a result, their racial vigour emasculated. On the other hand, the extreme right works towards the creation of its own version of a transnational elite, enforcing traditional family values and authoritarian, hierarchical societies domestically while eliciting the support of a like-minded globalised network. Hence the admiration that a whole range of extreme-right personalities often express towards President Putin (authoritarian extraordinaire), which depicts him not only as an exemplar of nationalism but as a potential leader of an alternative Eurasian empire. Currently, the Austrian Freedom Party (FPÖ), the Front National in France, Alternative for Germany, Ataka in Bulgaria, Jobbik in Hungary, the Northern League in Italy, Vlaams Belang in Belgium and Golden Dawn in Greece are among the extreme-right parties flirting with Putin and the idea of a 'Eurasian' power axis as a counter pole to the United States. Trump's positions on NATO and respect for Putin have of course been noted, particularly by Marine Le Pen.

On the other hand, it is the extra-parliamentary ultra-right that, by rejecting top-down national party structures in favour of less hierarchical, locally grounded networks, is concretising an anti-globalisation message. It is occupying those spaces evacuated by the mainstream political parties in rural areas, but also in manufacturing towns where the old community-support structures that used to characterise Europe's working-class life have collapsed. As many traditional functions are outsourced to private companies, local states are shrinking both in size and influence. This is something that the ultra-right senses and capitalises on, as witnessed by its emulation of social movement politics. In Italy, CasaPound, the self-styled 'fascists of the third millennium' that started out in 2003 in Rome and operate through cultural and students' associations, provides an innovative model. Loosely aligned since 2014 with the anti-immigration regional populists of the Northern League, the party's strategy has been to build up its membership through a movement for affordable housing, protesting at high rents and advocating squatters' rights.[11] At the other end of the fascist spectrum, the neo-Nazi NPD and the broader 'Nationalist Settlers' movement have focused on setting up communes in rural communities in the former GDR, taking up jobs in farming, the fire brigade and midwifery, acting as model citizens, sitting on the boards of schools and kindergartens, and even providing citizens' advice for those claiming welfare.[12] The formation of a 'welfare' and employment arm has been a trademark, too, of Golden Dawn, which, prior to the mass arrests of its leaders, ran blood banks and food kitchens (offering these services, needless to say, to white Greeks only), and visited factories and workplaces to count foreign workers and 'encourage' employers to hire Greeks instead. All this of course begs the question of who pays. Golden Dawn, communist trades unionists allege, not only made its money through blackmail, protection rackets and off-shore money laundering, but also had financial backing from employers in the zone of shipbuilding and repair at the Piraeus dockyards, which sought its services as an anti-trade union, anti-communist force in order to undermine the activities of the All-Workers Militant Inter-Union Front (PAME).

Countering Extremism: The Official Narrative

As every schoolchild knows, Hitler came to power using the tools of democracy to defeat democracy. For much of the extreme right in Europe today, the parliamentary road to power is certainly the dream. At the same time, the main goal of the extreme right is to alter the shape of national politics fundamentally, if not directly by winning majorities in elections then indirectly through participation in coalition governments in which it is hegemonic. Across Europe, electoral support for the mainstream centre right and centre left is crumbling. Herein lies the potential for the extreme right: to shake up and reconfigure politics, and establish itself in power.

At the time of writing, the situation is extremely fluid. On the one hand, there have been indications that, rather than lose control of local fiefdoms, centre-right regional politicians, and even social democrats (as in Austria's Burgenland), would be prepared to do deals or even enter into coalition governments with the extreme right. On the other hand, the election of Donald Trump in the United States, and the whole issue of the 'Kremlin's influence' and the 'Putin connection', may have put the fear of God into them, leading to a hardening of attitudes against the extreme right at the supranational level. An extreme right that builds its electoral base on anti-immigration, anti-minority rhetoric is one thing – its racism can be tolerated by them; the grievances of its electoral base can be pandered to. But an extreme right that is anti-Nato and pro-Russia, and may or may not have a standard-bearer in Trump (and Putin), is another matter. While the facts about Russian banks lending money to the FN and trips to Russia by extreme-right leaders at the invitation of political theorist Aleksandr Dugin cannot be disputed, the same is not true of the way in which the facts are assembled and over-egged to resurrect the Russian bogey-man and breathe new life into Cold War thinking. Against the backdrop of war in Ukraine and the tragedy of the proxy war between Russia and the United States in Syria, Cold War thinking has resurfaced. But today, these old anti-totalitarian frameworks (focusing on the twin evils of communism and fascism) are woven into the new state counter-extremism and counter-radicalisation programmes that have emerged in the context of the War on Terror.[13]

The European Commission has developed anti-extremism and counter-radicalisation initiatives as part of its counter-terrorism programme, first as a riposte to 'Islamist extremism', but now also embracing left and right as well as environmental activists and anti-fascists, whose resistance to corporate crimes or to fascism are all seen as part of a phenomenon of 'cumulative extremism'. Counter-extremism is now de rigueur, giving rise to a new professional class of experts attached to think tanks and university departments who vie for funding and influence. Suffice to say that the type of policy-orientated research engendered by these sorts of institutions proves very useful to all those who want to see the expansion of police powers and the intelligence services, as well as the criminalisation of resistance (to austerity measures or fascism, for instance). Though the defeat of Hillary Clinton and the reality of Brexit have shifted the goal posts somewhat, a meta-narrative has been established that leaves the state, or capital, out of any discussion of extremism. And if the biggest threat to society is seen to come from a generic extremism, then critical thinking is stalled. We become trained to understand fascism not as the convergence between affinities and affiliations at the periphery and centre of society, but as just another ideology for sale in the marketplace of extremisms. Nevertheless, contradictions abound. For example, in her 2015 New Year's address, Chancellor Angela Merkel declared that Germany would continue to accept refugees from Syria, and that the electorate should be wary of Pegida, for the hearts of its leaders were 'cold and often full of prejudice, even hate'. In parliament, as angry members of her proudly Christian Democratic Party looked on, she declared: 'Islam is a part of Germany.' It was a seeming volte-face – the clearest indication from a European leader for decades that racist movements should not be pandered to. And this from the author of European austerity and Greek humiliation, whose colleagues (particularly in Saxony), anxious about the advances of the AfD, had at the time urged her to negotiate with Pegida's leaders and acknowledge the grievances of its supporters. Merkel, the shrewdest and most stubborn of Europe's leaders, had no doubt cast her eye over Pegida's six-point programme. To the first chancellor of Germany from the former GDR, and the EU's lead negotiator with President Putin over the war in Ukraine (Merkel speaks fluent Russian), Pegida's demand that Berlin 'stop its warmongering against Russia' surely would have stood out. A few weeks later, a picture of Pegida's leader Lutz Bachmann posing on Facebook with a Hitler hairstyle and a toothbrush moustache was front-page news, and Bachmann was placed under investigation for sedition and incitement to racial hatred. Pegida split, as the so-called 'moderates' left, precipitating talk of further splits.

But to over-emphasise Merkel's unprecedented stance is to misunderstand both the nature of the threat and the nature of European society, in which parliamentary power is severely weakened, and mainstream parties have failed to maintain their roots in communities. The biggest threat to democracy lies in an unchecked, leviathan security state with its own meta-narrative of anti-extremism, the parameters of which protect the activities of the state and its security services from any reckoning.

The Challenge to the Left

It is in this Europe that the marriage of neoliberal austerity with racism is opening up Europe's old left–right fault lines – particularly in Greece, Spain and the UK. But the danger is increasingly obvious in central countries of Europe, too. And here the extreme right and ultra-right can operate most decisively at the local level, where anti-foreigner and authoritarian climates easily take hold in disconnected and discarded villages, towns and cities. Fascism starts by capturing public spaces – street, village or town – and turning them into native-only, foreigner-free zones. In an information society, the spaces that fascists seek to capture include television and social media, where they use free speech as the Trojan horse through which democratic societies can be infiltrated and undermined.

The emergence of Pegida is a warning to the left of the dangers and potential power of such political localism. For, despite the splits, since the outing of Bachmann and the formation of the movement Direct Democracy for Europe, the Saxony branches of the Christian Democrats and AfD have taken on aspects of Pegida's programme. As explained below (see Chapter 5), the AfD may have experienced setbacks, but it is still the most powerful far-right electoral bloc in the post-war period in Germany, and former Pegida supporters are joining its ranks. Bachmann, for his part, has left Germany, claiming political persecution, and set up shop on the Spanish island of Tenerife. Meanwhile Pegida itself is attempting to regroup as a Europe-wide movement. In France, for example, it has received some high-profile support from General Christian Piquemal, the seventy-five-year-old former head of the Foreign Legion and, until recently, president of the National Union of Parachutists.

And then there is the issue of the 'manipulation' of democratic vehicles themselves via right-wing populist movements. Since the British referendum on EU membership in June 2016, the EU's previous enthusiasm for more direct democracy, in the form of plebiscites, may have become more qualified. Referendums have been manipulated by the ultra-right ever since Hitler and Mussolini. The abuse of direct democracy continued in the post-war period, most notably with the 1971 Schwarzenbach referendum in Switzerland against Überfremdung (excess of foreigners), and the 2009 Swiss referendum banning minarets.[14]

Admittedly we are not there yet, but there is always the possibility that, as protests against austerity increase and the left is reinvigorated, the muscle and unfettered violence of the ultra-right could provide an alternative form of policing, silently tolerated and quickly disowned by the state. Southern European countries have a history to draw upon in this respect: death squads were part of the Spanish right's response to separatism in the Basque region and Catalonia, both during the dictatorship and immediately after. Today, the leaders of Spain's fascist parties have already upped the ante, declaring that they are willing to shoot the 'Catalan traitors' who launched a referendum on independence.

This collusion between the ultra-right and the state is not fanciful, but an existing threat. Greek lawyer Thanasis Kabayiannis, who edits the Jail Golden Dawn blog, points out, in the context of mounting evidence of collusion with the police and businesses, that Golden Dawn 'created battalions against their political opponents, and then they rented them out, to whoever wanted to rent them'. This chimes with the analysis offered in 1930 by Walter Benjamin on the relationship between the state and private militias. In *Theories of German Fascism*, Benjamin warned that the nationalist paramilitary groups (*Freikorps*) that flourished in the inter-war period would prove very useful to sections of the military (*Reichswehr*) and other vested interests hostile to democracy in the Weimar Republic. They were nothing less than 'mercenary hordes ... available for hire at any time, like rice or turnips, by arrangement through private agencies', he wrote.

The ultra-right might be used today, as it was under classical fascism, as a tool for the disciplining and intimidation of the left. For instance, it was in the interests of the Greek oligarchs (the shipping magnates, the bosses of the energy and construction groups, and football club owners) to encourage the rise of a far-right political party with a paramilitary wing. It was a kind of political safety net against the radical left, the election programme of which promised to oppose not only the life-sucking anti-austerity measures imposed on Greece by the Troika (the European Commission, the European Central Bank and the IMF), but also the systemic corruption and cronyism endemic within Greek political culture itself.

The pattern of collusion, direct or indirect, between the military, the police and the intelligence services, or a combination of all three, and the ultra-right can be detected not just in Greece, but in other regions of Europe. And here lies the biggest challenge for the left. Fascism does not hatch eggs only on the margins of a society; it breeds within existing authoritarian structures, within those spaces most shielded from public scrutiny, such as the police and intelligence services, which provide the perfect incubators. Europe's law enforcement agencies were never fully democratised in the post-war period. But the massive expansion of criminal justice as a result of the War on Terror, the securitisation of migration, the militarisation of public-order policing, the criminalisation of poverty, and the incarceration of the poor and the mentally ill have increased anti-democratic trends exponentially. That is why the attempts by NSU-Watch and Golden Dawn Watch to prise open the secrets of the security services, the military and other elites are of vital importance. Many of Syriza's pre-election pledges – to demilitarise the Hellenic police and disband its neo-Nazi elements; to create oversight mechanisms for the police and the military; to disband Operation Xenios Zeus and close down the detention centres – have still to be met. This is an undertaking that demands realisation.

Conflict is growing in Europe, but there are signs that the anti-fascist tradition can provide a counter-force to the ultra-right. The murder by Breivik of so many idealistic anti-racist youngsters with an internationalist vision on Oslo's Utøya Island was the first sign that political violence had returned to Europe. Die Linke in Germany, Syriza in Greece, a whole host of left civil society groups in Spain, and pro-Palestinian and migrant and refugee rights activists in other European countries, are now being subjected to systematic political violence from the right. But today the left faces the added burden posed by an EU-wide counter-extremism industry which, in treating left resistance to this political violence as just another form of extremism, is making it easier for states to criminalise anti-fascists.

II.

The Structural Shift
to the Right

3

Establishing Norms: The Cultural Revolution from the Right

The threat to representative democracies from authoritarianism and fascism does not start or end with the extreme and ultra-right. On the contrary, the centre right, drawing on a cultural conservatism that has deep roots in European economic and political thought and within its various nationalisms, has not faltered when it comes to the attack on liberal values. Illiberalism runs like a thread through the right's economic theories, from Anglo-Saxon laissez-faire through to neoliberalism, or the ordoliberalism of Germany and the European Central Bank. The EU's embrace of neoliberalism, and now austerity, has strengthened European authoritarianism, both at a member-state level and within the EU, where the powerful core countries set the agenda. Thus, the German finance minister, Wolfgang Schäuble, acting as though the EU were an empire and he its domineering overlord, could tell the Greek left party, Syriza, that its democratic mandate secured in the general election of 2015 on the back of calls for debt relief had no meaning, as '[e]lections change nothing. There are rules'.

Nor did the unelected Troika – the European Commission, European Central Bank and IMF – blink an eye as it vetoed democracy in Greece, turning that country, in William Keegan's words, into a 'browbeaten and humiliated vassal state seething with resentment'. Deficit reduction may pose as a fiscal necessity, but it is much more than mere economics: it is the fiscal means towards a political end. Thus, the undermining of redistributive policies in the economic sphere has been accompanied by the rolling back of progressive gains in the social sphere. Under cover of austerity, the right has deepened its aggressive raid on post-war egalitarian and inclusive social policies. All those who question the concentration of political power within a corporate and financial elite, or continue to champion the cause of a 'social Europe', are derided by the right. On the other hand, even as it implements austerity, the right can assume the cloak of progressive politics, declaring itself the voice of working people. The behaviour of right-wing politicians, like former Conservative British chancellor George Osborne, provides a clear example. In summer 2015, Osborne used his budget announcement of the so-called 'living wage' as a rhetorical point of departure from which to argue that the Conservatives were the party of working people, even as he attempted to cut tax credits to the working poor.

Yet rampant inequality and employment insecurity are growing. With sections of the middle classes now fearful for the future of their children, the seductive neoliberal pull of radical individualism and freedom via consumerism is losing its hold. While a resort to nationalism, patriotism and pride in the military provides one way for the mainstream right to enforce order and authority, it is not without risks. Notwithstanding public support for anti-terrorist laws to deal with 'Islamic' terrorism, illiberal aspects of state power are becoming more generalised, and therefore more open to contestation. If order and authority are to be maintained in the face of the erosion of the social safety net – and without even the dream of social mobility to mitigate the hardships – then the state must become more coercive, the exercise of state power more brutal. What follows is an attempt to explain the mechanics and dynamics of modern illiberalism, showing how old tropes inherited from the cultural conservative, authoritarian and colonial traditions are woven into current themes. Within this dynamic, a coterie of New Right intellectuals, has been extremely influential in changing attitudes to cultural and political pluralism, thereby breathing new life into old ideas associated with the Conservative Revolution in the period just after the First World War. The New Right proceeds through an intellectual narrative that promotes culture wars and patriot games, with the ultimate goal of transforming the way in which race, race relations and human rights are discussed, pushing back the civil and social rights won by black people and ethnic minorities in historic struggles against racism and discrimination in the post-war period.

Patriot Games, Culture Wars and the Attack on Multiculturalism

In a speech in Cheltenham in April 2009, David Cameron, then leader of the opposition, announced that the Conservative Party would fight the 2010 general election in the UK on 'Labour economic irresponsibility', the 'Labour debt crisis' and the 'culture of profligacy'.[1] Promising deep cuts in public expenditure, low taxes and low interest rates, Cameron, with a nod to the economic liberalism and productive parsimony of Adam Smith and David Hume, declared: 'the age of irresponsibility is giving way to the age of austerity'. Six years later, in the May 2015 general election, the Conservatives won a narrow majority and a second term of office, unencumbered by the Liberal Democrat partners in their coalition of the previous five years. It was a result that baffled outside observers. How could the British electorate vote against its self-interest, they asked, pointing out that the Conservative programme not only penalised the overwhelming majority of the population for the banking crisis, but redistributed wealth away from the working and middle classes towards financial elites.

Part of the answer lies in the way in which right-wing patriot games and culture wars – enacted via discussions of immigration and multiculturalism, national identity and terrorism, as well as southern European economic profligacy – have been waged across Europe. Central to the ways in which electorates have been conned into voting against their true interests has been the Europe-wide assault on multiculturalism, which has been blamed for the creation of 'parallel societies' and the undermining of European laws, languages and traditions. Understood primarily as an attack on Muslim communities across Europe, anti-multiculturalism has paved the way for right-wing ideas about the integral or organic nation to resurface. This has proved very useful to traditional elites associated with English, Castilian and pan-German nationalism, which seek to impose their hegemonic vision of the nation upon multi-nation states and pluralist societies. Hence, the seeds from which the right's assault on progressive politics would grow were sown well before the financial crisis.

Already, in the immediate aftermath of 9/11, a number of right-wing politicians, while not going as far as the Italian prime minister Silvio Berlusconi in declaring the 'superiority' of Western civilisation, were making statements criticising multiculturalism. Crucially, aside from Berlusconi's, these were made mostly by New Right commentators, along with the leaders of electoral anti-immigration movements such as the Danish People's Party and List Pim Fortuyn. The mainstream right, though critical, distanced itself from Berlusconi, as well as from Samuel Huntington's 'clash of civilisations' thesis (see below).

By 2011, things had moved on. Leading Norwegian Conservative Torbjørn Røe Isaksen denounced 'the naive liberal ideology that people can live together in peace and freedom if they just understand each other well enough'.[2] Throughout that year, centre-right (and some centre-left) politicians in Austria, Belgium, France, Germany, Denmark, the Netherlands, Norway and the United Kingdom took aim, in speeches heavily trailed in the media, at what David Cameron had described as the 'state doctrine of multiculturalism'. Cameron, in a speech at a security conference in Munich, argued that this doctrine had 'encouraged different cultures to live separate lives, apart from each other and the mainstream', leading to the 'weakening of our collective identity'. The resulting 'passively tolerant society' needs to be replaced by a 'much more active muscular liberalism', he said. In this, he was repeating the message delivered earlier by the German chancellor Angela Merkel, who declared in Potsdam in October 2010 that the multicultural society had 'utterly failed', that the 'multikulti' concept – where people would 'live side-by-side' happily – did not work. Sharing the podium with her in Potsdam was Horst Seehofer, the leader of the Christian Social Union (CSU – the CDU's sister-party in Bavaria), who declared that multiculturalism was dead, adding that the right was committed to a 'leading culture' (*Leitkultur*).

It was a view shared by the outgoing Belgian prime minister Yves Leterme and other conservative leaders, from Dutch deputy prime minister Maxine Verhagen and Danish Liberal Party immigration minister Søren Pind (a former advisory board member of the Danish Free Press Society, a key think tank for the counter-jihadi movement) to French conservative former president Nicolas Sarkozy. During a television interview, and using a characteristically impatient tone, Sarkozy declared: 'We do not want ... a society where communities coexist side by side. If you come to France, you accept to melt into a single community, which is the national community, and if you do not want to accept that, you cannot be welcome in France.' Greek and Spanish politicians, bolstered by the anti-Islam, anti-multicultural discourse of the Catholic and Orthodox clergy, have also joined the attack in recent years. It was all these politicians who paved the way, several years later, for the self-declared champion of 'illiberal democracy', Hungarian prime minister Viktor Orbán, to challenge a coordinated European approach to the Syrian refugee crisis.

Orbán declared in the summer of 2015 that the only way to protect the Hungarian people from 'dying out' was by opposing the 'multicultural society brought about by immigration', stress-ing the importance of the Christian-national idea as a bulwark against the Islamisation of Europe.[3] European politicians who had shown no restraint in attacking multiculturalism in 2011 were now outflanked by Orbán, who – with the support of Bavarian prime minister Seehofer – linked anti-multicultural-ism to a defence of a crusader Christianity. Orbán emerged as the leader of the European parliamentary extreme right against the 'moral imperialism' of Angela Merkel, whom he attacked for her handling of the refugee crisis at a summit in Brussels after travelling via Bavaria, where he was hosted by the CSU and hailed by Seehofer as 'Europe's border guard captain' who 'deserves support, not criticism'. The outsider Orbán, echoing Martin Luther, declared that he would not retreat, as 'I can only say, here I stand. Cannot do otherwise.'[4] According to him, 'We are experiencing the end of a spiritual-intellectual era. The era of liberalism.' Later, at a CDU conference in Karlsruhe, Merkel saw off the rebellion in her own centre-right ranks by repeating her support for Germany's leading culture and opposition to the 'grand delusion' of multiculturalism.

The Centrality of the New Right

From late 2010 onwards, Merkel and Cameron and the par-liamentary right reset the policy agenda; but, in so doing, they drew on an earlier critique of multiculturalism. Since the 1970s, in response to left, civil rights and anti-racist gains, a loose com-munity of political journalists, philosophers, writers, academics and politicians, broadly referred to as the New Right, had been attempting to redefine the way 'race' was discussed. Denying any support for the notion of racial superiority, the New Right stressed cultural differences, human nature, human instinct and the need to preserve 'our way of life' to justify their assault on multiculturalism. New Right arguments were to gain ground in the 1980s and 1990s, but, critically, international events such as the end of apartheid in 1994, as well as the moral force of anti-racist movements across Europe, established a counter-narrative to the advancement of racist positions under cover of cultural critique. It was the Al-Qaeda attacks in New York and Washington on 11 September 2001 and the popularisation of neoconservative Samuel Huntington's 'clash of civilisations' thesis (which stated that, in a post–Cold War world, global conflict would be cultural rather than ideological) that changed the balance.[5] Many New Right authors achieved celebrity status virtually overnight, while others waged a war of position, capturing key spaces in the print media. Such commentators provided the intellectual hinterland for the broader right's assault on progressive politics. Their popular appeal lay in their ability to speak to the *ennui* of middle-class malcontents and drive their latent racial and religious prejudices into a fever of cultural enmity.

The New Right's stated aim was to stretch the limits of public debate. Its goal was to revitalise European right elites and reshape conservatism in its own image. With a nod to Gramsci's theory of cultural hegemony, on the one hand,[6] and Carl Schmitt's instruction that 'real power' lies 'in the ability to set the norms and to decide when they apply and to whom', on the other, they sought their own cultural revolution from the right. In establishing new norms, the New Right was to exceed all expectations, speeding up a process whereby the values associated with social democracy were to disintegrate from within. For its own reasons, including the embrace of 'humanitarian interventionism' in the Middle East (as epitomised by Tony Blair) and support for the neoliberal project to shrink the welfare state, social democracy bought into the New Right agenda. Social democrats began to use legitimate progressive criticisms of culturalist and ethnicist government policies (which could result in segregation and communal-style local politics) to justify this shift and win the support of some feminists and gay rights activists for an attack on diversity per se.

In the 1970s and 1980s, the New Right (particularly in the

UK, France, Germany and Italy) was never a single, unified force.[7] Nevertheless, its influence could be clearly seen in the activities of a number of think tanks associated with journals such as the *Salisbury Review*, *Junge Freiheit*, *Nouvelle École* and *Éléments – pour la civilisation européenne*. But today, despite their undoubtedly sharing a lineage with the New Right thinkers who emerged in the 1970s, it is even less clear what or who constitutes the second wave of the New Right. This is partly because its voices are more diverse, but it is also due to changes in the New Right's tone and defining narrative. By and large, its tenor is no longer that of the rational Western man foregrounding issues of human behaviour. Instead, the tone is far more self-consciously emotional and literary – drawing not so much on the study of human biology as the study of human culture and civilisation. In what follows, I use 'New Right' as an umbrella term encompassing a number of overlapping tendencies across a spectrum of right-wing illiberal thought united around a core of common beliefs (such as hostility to concepts like universalism, pluralism and equality), as well as a polemic against the Western self-hatred that arises out of left-wing cultural relativism.

The New Right, then, may have been less vocal towards the end of the last century, but it certainly did not disappear. After the events of 9/11, as anti-terrorist laws were introduced in response to what Tony Blair described in a speech in his Sedgefield constituency in March 2004 as a 'real and existential threat' that needs to be 'fought, whatever the cost', conspiracy theories and apocalyptic narratives about Muslims and the Arab world began to have greater purchase.[8] Suddenly, it was boom time for the New Right. One idea it floated was that of Eurabia – the notion, first popularised by Bat Ye'or (a pseudonym), that Europe is being colonised by the Arab world and forced into an attitude of *dhimmitude*, or Western subjection to Islam.[9] Right-wing and neoconservative think tanks and foundations such as the Henry Jackson Society, the Danish Free Press Society and the Human Rights Service in Norway began to flirt with the

Eurabia theme. At the same time, a whole new literary genre was emerging, those who peddled the theme being celebrated in the mainstream media as prophets and authors of the latest literary situation. The titillating titles, often written in a confessional, popular style, reflect the superficial and narcissistic content of this particular genre: *Infidel: My Life* and *Nomad: From Islam to America: A Personal Journey through the Clash of Civilizations*, both by Ayaan Hirsi Ali; *Hurrah! We Capitulate: On the Desire to Cave In*, by Henryk M. Broder; *The Rage and the Pride*, *The Force of Reason* and *Oriana Fallaci Interviews Herself: The Apocalypse*, all by the late Oriana Fallaci; *But the Greatest of These is Freedom: The Consequences of Immigration in Europe*, by Norwegian anti-immigration feminist Hege Storhaug. *The Unhappy Identity* and *The French Suicide: The Forty Years That Have Defined France* were offered up to the public by the French celebrity writers Alain Finkielkraut and Éric Zemmour, a *Le Figaro* columnist, who, after the ISIS terrorist outrage in Paris on 13 November 2015, told the RTL radio station: 'Instead of bombing Raqqa [in Syria], France should bomb Molenbeek [in Brussels].'

Foundations and Innovations

Whatever their supposed innovation or iconoclasm, their perspectives and much of their language are not altogether new. Their ideas overlap with those of the anti-liberal thinkers writing in the period after the First World War, particularly Oswald Spengler, whose *Decline of the West* appeared in 1922, and Carl Schmitt (often referred to as the 'Nazi jurist'), who joined the National Socialists in 1933, was arrested at the end of the war, but evaded prosecution at the Nuremberg Trials and was later influential on both left and right with *Dictatorship* (1921), *Political Theology* (1922) and *The Concept of the Political* (1927).[10]

In addition to Schmitt and Spengler's association with the Conservative Revolution movement in Europe (which, in

Germany, provided the intellectual climate for the triumph of National Socialism, and Schmitt's direct association with it), both are also foundational thinkers within modern cultural conservatism. They were writing at a time when European society, though convinced of its racial superiority, 'was haunted by the spectre of its own degeneration'.[11] Since today only diehard neo-Nazis make the case for racial superiority, today's New Right substitutes racial with civilisational hierarchies – and their ideas have gained traction because of the cultural racism that has accompanied the War on Terror. Schmitt's writings on constitutional theory and his critique of liberalism and the politics of compromise have provided a rich legacy for the right, who draw in particular on his friend/foe distinction in the field of politics, his assertion that 'enmity' is the distinctive feature of political existence and his support for untrammelled executive power in the face of an emergency. Schmitt's theories, once taken up by Franco and Salazar to justify dictatorship, provide an intellectual foundation for those who seek a more authoritarian turn in the style of government. Professor David Luban, an expert in legal ethics, noted the '"Schmittian" character of the Bush administration's constitutional arguments', regarding Schmitt as an influence on US law officials John Yoo and Alberto R. Gonzales in the drawing up of the torture memos and the legal authorisation of 'enhanced interrogation techniques'.[12]

On the other hand, the gift handed down to a generation of New Right thinkers by the meta-historian Oswald Spengler (whose *Decline of the West* was the literary sensation of its day) lies more in Spengler's cultural despair and authorial voice. There is an obvious link between this cultural pessimism and today's celebrity prophets of doom who rail against the corrosive and devouring forces of liberalism that leave the self-hating Occident supine in the face of the self-confident brute force of a barbaric Orient.

Cultural conservatism, then, has been one of the defining influences on a literary genre defined by civilisational pessimism and apocalyptic visions about immigrant invasion and national disintegration. This is nowhere more true than in France, where New Right public intellectuals have been all the rage since the mid 2000s. While not (for the most part) publicly claiming allegiance to the FN, such right-wing celebrities undoubtedly created the intellectual framework that was to deliver Marine Le Pen's 10.6 million votes in the second round of the French presidential elections in 2017 – the highest share of the vote gained by a far-right candidate in Europe since the Second World War. While 10.6 million backed Le Pen, the independent candidate Emmanuel Macron, with 66.1 per cent of the vote, easily secured the presidency. France's best-known New Right fiction writer is Michel Houellebecq. His novel *Submission*, set in France in 2022, when the country is run by an Islamist president courtesy of an anti-FN alliance, was an instant success when it was published in January 2015. It has been compared to Jean Raspail's racist political satire of 1973, *The Camp of the Saints* (incidentally a favourite of Donald Trump's chief strategist, Steve Bannon), which also deals with Europe's impotence, this time in the face of an invasion of immigrant Indians. Another new-right celebrity is TV intellectual and *Le Figaro* columnist Éric Zemmour, who, in his bestselling nonfiction polemic of 2014, *The French Suicide: The Forty Years that Defeated France*, argued against the 'halalisation' of France characterised by the creation of 'Islamic Republics in certain neighbourhoods', and claimed not only that French society has become too feminine, but that the Vichy regime was misunderstood. More open in his support for Marine Le Pen is prominent gay writer Renaud Camus who, in 2010, echoing the Eurabia theme, coined the term '*le grand remplacement*' to describe the colonisation of France by Muslim immigrants from the Middle East and North Africa, which threatens to 'mutate' the country and its culture permanently. The French 'neo-reactionaries', as they are dubbed by their critics, have been vocal since at least 2007, when the journal *Causeur* was founded by the formerly left-wing journalist Elisabeth Lévy and the historian Gil Mihaely, who argued that the journal was needed because mainstream publications were too scared to discuss issues such as immigration and national identity. Well before the November 2015 ISIS-inspired terrorist attacks in France, the New Right dominated the airwaves and the newspaper stands, fuelling debates about national identity and immigration to the benefit, ultimately, of the Front National.

Neoconservatism, Muscular Liberalism and Cold War Frameworks

Cultural conservatism has provided a rich vein for the New Right. But unlike the emotive Eurabia genre, other frameworks associated with neoconservativism (the clash of civilisations) and aggressive, muscular liberalism (the new totalitarianism) hold out the promise, at least, of political analysis. Neoconservative frameworks suggesting that Muslims en masse cling to inherently anti-modern characteristics held sway until the end of George W. Bush's presidency. Since then, as Arun Kundnani has persuasively argued, rightists and liberals have self-consciously embraced Cold War frameworks, arguing that 'Islamism', like Stalinism and fascism, represents a new totalitarianism to which the correct response is a cultural war, with tough measures against those who hold on to this 'evil ideology', accompanied by a political contest for the hearts and minds of ordinary Muslims.[13] What both liberals and neoconservatives share, according to Kundnani, is a 'discourse of ideological warfare'. Thus, despite their attempt to appear more scholarly and serious, European neoconservatives and their liberal and right-wing offshoots fall back on culturally conservative frameworks, emphasising a need to maintain civilisational vigour and contest the growing effeminisation of society. While the Henry Jackson Society in the UK is often associated with neoconservative frameworks (its associate director, Douglas Murray, being the author of *Neoconservatism: Why We Need It*), so too is Policy Exchange, founded by former Conservative justice minister Michael Gove, who, in the polemical text *Celsius 7/7*, argued that Western self-hatred and a lack of moral clarity had made us blind to the totalitarianism of Islamic fundamentalism. Neoconservative and/or culturally conservative thinkers, whose preoccupations most often overlap with a vigorous defence of Israel and Zionism, have added a number of seemingly less populist, less confessional titles to the New Right literary genre. These include *Les Territoires Perdue de la République: Antisémitisme, racism et sexism en milieu scolaire (The Lost Territories of the Republic: Anti-Semitism, Racism and Sexism in the Educational Sphere)*, by Georges Bensoussan, the Holocaust historian and editor-in-chief of *La Revue d'Histoire de la Shoah*; *Reflections on the Revolution in Europe: Immigration, Islam and the West*, by *Financial Times* columnist Christopher Caldwell; and *Oikofobie*, an attack on non-Western art as well as modernism by the darling of the Dutch New Right, Thierry Baudet, founder of the electoral party Forum for Democracy. Undoubtedly, one of the most politically influential neoconservatives of this generation has been Flemming Rose, who, as cultural editor of the Danish newspaper *Jyllands-Posten*, commissioned a series of Mohammed cartoons. Rose went on to write *Tyranny of Silence: How One Cartoon Ignited a Global Debate on the Future of Free Speech*, published in English by the Cato Institute and financed partly by the US libertarian Koch brothers.[14]

The Centre-Left Assimilates New-Right Ideas

We have also witnessed a movement of thinkers from the left of the political spectrum over to the New Right. But this is not just a question of individual conversion to the New Right cause. The broader picture is one in which the New Right sets the terms of the debate, particularly on multiculturalism and Islam, and centre-left thinkers, with weak or nonexistent anti-racist principles, creep over into New Right territory. So, on the one hand, you have the intellectual journey from left to right of figures like Elisabeth Lévy, who started out in the 1980s as a socialist and columnist for the anti-racist and Mitterand-supporting newspaper, the *Globe*, before becoming disillusioned over immigration and eventually founding the French New Right's most influential journal, *Causeur*, in 2007. The movement of others across the political spectrum has been equally tortuous, many not even conscious that they have strayed far from the (politically and culturally pluralist) social-democratic camp, as they attempt to push it towards an anti-immigration and anti-multiculturalist agenda. The Dutch publicist and social democrat Paul Scheffer, in his influential essay '*Het multiculturele drama*' (The Multicultural Disaster [2000]), was among the first to blame the cultural relativism of the liberal elite for failures in integration, arguing that multiculturalism was hindering integration into the basic values of Dutch society. Similarly, in the UK, the founding editor of *Prospect*, David Goodhart, remained in the Labour fold while incorporating New Right arguments. In his 2004 essay, 'Too Diverse', Goodhart argued that entitlement to welfare should be clearly aligned with belonging to a shared British culture, and that liberals faced a choice between the welfare state and diversity.[15] He remained director of the centre-left think tank Demos until 2016, when he finally moved on to the neoconservative Policy Exchange, where he currently heads up its Demography, Immigration and Integration Unit. In his latest book, *The Road to Somewhere: The Populist Revolt and the Future of Politics*, Goodhart calls for an understanding of 'majority grievances' which he argues represents 'decent populism', not racism.

In the German-speaking world it was, fittingly, also a centre-left figure, the Social Democrat Thilo Sarrazin, who provided the lightning-rod for a deeply reactionary debate about multiculturalism and welfare, and became the darling of the right. In 2010, the first issue of the glossy New Right magazine *Compact*, edited by Jürgen Elsässer – himself a former editor of the left-wing magazine *Konkret* who helped found the anti-Deutsche movement before completely migrating to the New Right – featured as its cover a photo of Sarrazin with the headline: 'The Next Federal Chancellor?' Sarrazin's *Deutschland Shafft Sich Ab: Wie Wir Unser Land Aufs Spiel Setzen* (Germany Abolishes Itself: How We Are Playing with Our Future) sparked off a nationwide media debate about 'flawed integration' and 'feeble multiculturalism'. In his polemic, Sarrazin warned that Germany's national survival – its ethno-cultural essence, no less – was in mortal danger, its future demographic threatened by the higher reproduction rates and lower intelligence of a cultural–religious category, 'Muslim migrants'. Michael Meng has done sterling service in dissecting Sarrazin's thesis. He finds it replete with cultural and biological racism, and a narrative driven by 'an ethnocultural anxiety about national survival and an elitist concern about the preservation of an educated upper class'.[16] Yet Sarrazin's diatribe was to become one of the most popular books on politics by a German-language author in a decade, making him a multi-millionaire.

Sarrazin was influenced by the US social scientist Charles Murray, a fellow of the neoconservative American Enterprise Institute who had worked with the US military to develop counter-insurgency programmes in Southeast Asia. In 1994, Murray co-authored, with psychologist Richard Herrnstein, *The Bell Curve: Intelligence and Class Structure in American Life*, which resurrected the claims of disreputable race theorists about racial differences in IQ. The initial response to Sarrazin's book was one of horror at a similar resort to genetic arguments, not least the declaration that 'all Jews share the same gene'. But as the public embraced Sarrazin, scientific racism was forgiven, *Der Spiegel* commenting that 'the tome may be full of inaccuracies, but it has struck a nerve'.[17] Centre-right politicians likewise distanced themselves from Sarrazin's social-Darwinist views, but aligned themselves with the message, arguing that, when it came to issues of multiculturalism and integration (of Muslims in particular), Sarrazin was making valid points. Extreme-right politicians in German-speaking countries such as Switzerland

and Austria sympathised with the 'hunted Sarrazin'. Crucially, in policy terms, he also drew the support of Austria's centre-right interior minister Maria Fekter, of the Austrian People's Party (ÖVP), who was at that time busy recalibrating integration policies around an assimilationist model. Fekter went further than any other senior conservative in identifying herself with Sarrazin, saying she felt 'confirmed' by the debate he had initiated. While Merkel initially described Sarrazin's thesis as 'not helpful', she later used it for her own political advantage, introducing a strident assimilationist tone into the debate on integration in her Potsdam speech (see above), for which she received a standing ovation.

The Impact on Policy: From Integration to Assimilation

The New Right's political rhetoric against multiculturalism has been extremely influential in shifting the terms of debate, and has also had a bearing on social policy, particularly in the field of integration, equalities and combating discrimination. Cultural–religious explanations for economic and social marginalisation had already become the dominant framework for policymaking in the post-9/11 period. A monocultural approach (based on integration into British values, French values, and so on) was held up as a necessary security blanket against terrorism and radicalisation. Since 2011, when multiculturalism has been described as a 'grand illusion', the path has also opened up for governments to abandon any positive duty to combat racism and discrimination through an equalities agenda. Integration policies ('unity in diversity') have been recalibrated around what Andrew Ryder has characterised as a 'one size fits all' menu of policy interventions ('unity in sameness').[18] At the same time, proponents of the mainstream political agenda are keen to distance themselves, at least nominally, from the electoral challenge of the racist right, avoiding the overtly racist language and strident bigotry of the 1960s and 1970s, when the British Conservative politician Enoch Powell talked of 'alien hordes' and called for the 'induced repatriation' of Asian and African-Caribbean immigrants from the UK, and the Swiss politician James Schwarzenbach launched a referendum on Überfremdung (too many foreigners), which was only narrowly defeated. Overt racism based on skin colour is unlawful under EU directives. Nevertheless, the idea that racial justice is a cause worth pursuing through targeted policy approaches to end discrimination finds far less favour in Europe today. At best, European leaders are concerned about 'fairness', 'equality of opportunity', 'subtle discrimination' and 'unconscious bias' (all phrases used by David Cameron in an October 2015 *Guardian* article) in university applications or at the higher end of the job market, since a culturally diverse, highly skilled workforce is an advantage in the globalised economies of the finance and IT sectors – particularly when governments are eager to woo foreign direct investment from countries like China and India. Nevertheless, as the Institute of Race Relations' Jenny Bourne has outlined in relation to the UK how, the anti-multiculturalism discourse has eroded any respect for difference.[19] In the process, European governments have 'come full circle', free to return to the post-war philosophy of explicit cultural assimilation. While it may be true that not all European politicians will openly use a term like assimilation, the 'mainstreaming', 'uniforming' or 'colour-blind' approach that is now a central preoccupation of the right is identical with assimilation. As Sivanandan notes, it is 'a subsumption of the minority under the majority'. Once again, a shift in policy, this time away from integration as a two-way process (in which the majority society simultaneously looks to end discrimination), attests to the hegemony that the New Right has achieved in shaping the agenda, this time on the battleground of diversity and equality.

But then, in many countries, discourses about national identity encapsulating norms long in the making were porous to New Right ideas. For example, in France, a monocultural approach has long been national ideology, favoured by both

Gaullists and socialists in the 'indivisible Republic' with its tradition of civic individualism, where the individual participates in politics as a citizen, free of community or ethnic ties. France is a country that does not accept that it has ethnic, religious or linguistic minorities, as evidenced by its reservation to Article 27 (minority rights) of the International Covenant on Civil and Political Rights. In France, it is not only illegal to collect statistics on ethnicity or race, but everyone is meant to submerge their regional or ethnic identity into the one common identity of the Republic. But in different ways, too, the tunnel vision inherent in the Scandinavian social-democratic 'one human race' approach to integration contains an ethnocentrism which, by denying race as a social construct, betrays New Right influence. This point is not lost on African–Swedish associations that have had to contend, in recent years, with the white chauvinism of centre-right and centre-left politicians alike. They have defended the indefensible, justifying, for instance, the tradition of describing a popular Swedish dessert as a 'negro balls' cake, or laughing off an incident in 2012 when, at a public function, the culture minister cut into the genital area of a cake depicting a stereotypical black woman. From a different end of the political spectrum, conservatives in Germany have, since the 1990s, been attached to the notion of *Leitkultur*, the political idea that immigrants have to assimilate into the leading culture and incorporate its values. It is a rigid monocultural approach that denies multicultural realities, and its influence can be clearly seen today in the ten-point set of guidelines issued by interior minister Thomas de Maizière, which includes an ear for Bach and Goethe, a willingness to shake hands, and pride in Europe. Most disappointingly, it is in the UK, the Netherlands and Sweden, countries which had been more receptive to ideas of racial equality – even, in the case of the UK, officially recognising institutional racism – that the abandonment of more progressive frameworks has been most pronounced.

What impact has all this had on the ground? In 2000, the EU brought in the Racial Equality Directive, following a strong campaign by equality bodies that set up the Starting Line Group for a specific directive outlawing discrimination on grounds of race or ethnicity. Other anti-discrimination measures, such as the Employment Equality Directives, which placed member-states under an obligation to put in place efficient remedies to tackle discrimination, were passed in 2010. The directives have never been properly enforced, largely because inadequate resources are given to their public enforcement through national and EU agencies. But the 'mainstreaming' approach adopted throughout most of Europe, accompanied by austerity-driven cuts to legal aid, has weakened the ability to enforce anti-discrimination measures by reducing resources still further. National and regional bodies tasked with combating racial equality have been refashioned around a general equality remit. Hence the morphing of the European Union Monitoring Centre Against Racism and Xenophobia into the Fundamental Rights Agency, and the Commission for Racial Equality (CRE) in the UK into the Equality and Human Rights Commission, with severe budgetary and personnel cuts. (The UK body, for instance, had its budget cut from £70 million in 2009/10 to £17 million in 2014/15.) This policy approach, facilitated by politicians from across the political spectrum, has been characterised by Lord Herman Ouseley, a former head of the CRE, as 'equalities high-level blue-sky waffling'.[20]

At the same time, law centres and local anti-discrimination NGOs, as well as victim-support schemes, have been cut back in countries where they had previously enjoyed subsidies. In Germany, government support for independent schemes to support the victims of racist and fascist violence do not enjoy the levels of financial support given to the perpetrators of that violence via the Exit counter-radicalisation programmes for neo-Nazis and other former extremists (see Chapter 6). In the UK, the 'mainstreaming' or 'colour-blind' approach to equality has led to a widespread loss of expertise in local government departments, which has had particularly harsh consequences for Roma, Traveller and Gypsy communities. In Poland, the

Council Against Racial Discrimination, Xenophobia and Intolerance has been closed down; and in Spain, the Popular Party government cut back the Permanent Observatory on Immigration (OPI) and the Spanish Observatory on Racism and Xenophobia (Oberaxe), with devastating effects for communities that suffer discrimination.

Common-Sense Racism

But then, for the right, EU anti-discrimination laws represent unnecessary red tape. If the free market discriminates, it discriminates in favour of the 'strivers' not the 'shirkers'; the 'invisible hand' of the free market rewards merit and ambition. For neoliberals, 'social justice' is not about 'securing livelihoods and participation for all, but rewarding efficiency and motivation'.[21] Within this mind set, the role for the state, if any, is to act as a referee, an enabler, ensuring fair play through a few mechanistic measures such as name-free application forms, to mitigate 'unconscious bias'. In 'post-racial' Europe, racial disparities, if acknowledged at all, are blamed on those who cannot adjust to modern realities because they choose to dwell in the poverty of their own culture. In the run-up to the 2017 general elections in the Netherlands, centre-right prime minister Mark Rutte took out a full-page letter in several national newspapers in which he criticised those who refuse to assimilate into Dutch values, and implied that immigrants should stop complaining about discrimination but 'fight their way in'. Brexiteer Iain Duncan Smith, the former British secretary of state for work and pensions, resorts, unconsciously perhaps, to the language of the late-nineteenth-century social Darwinists when he argues that we must look to 'the dysfunctional base' of the poor if we are to understand poverty. If society's strivers are the true victims of society's shirkers (in social Darwinist terms, the 'brutalised residuum' or the 'improvident poor'), then the white majority are equally victims of racialised minorities' unending demands.

A whole lexicon of white victimhood has grown up, with its everyday fables and fictions about resentful minorities and rampaging migrants comprising a new common-sense racism, where the decent, civilised and law-abiding majority emerge as the victims of legally privileged minorities and liberal elites who embrace diversity within a philosophy of 'unbridled multiculturalism which privileges difference over community cohesion'.[22] No longer to be harangued and made to feel guilty by the non-natives, or hemmed in by powerful taboos – or to feel, in Cameron's words, 'so cautious, frankly even fearful, to stand up to them' for 'fear of causing offence or being branded a racist' – muscular majorities, confident in the superiority of the dominant culture, can stop behaving like 'naive liberals'; they can stand up to their political and cultural enemies.

The Enabler State

The New Right ideological push, and states' policy reversals, cannot, of course, be divorced from the way in which states were changing their role as the post-war welfare consensus broke down. At the same time as the New Right was waging what could be termed its war of position, 'the tectonic plates beneath the state' were shifting 'from serving the nation to serving the market'.[23] Under the impact of the neoliberal drive to liberate corporations from any government regulation, to sell off state-owned enterprises, goods and services to private investors, and to dismantle state bureaucracies that delivered welfare by outsourcing services to contractors, the market, in the words of Sivanandan, began to drive society.

In such a radically reconstructed state, representative democracies are far weaker, and parliaments less open to scrutiny as power congeals around lobby organisations, quangos, private companies, think tanks and GONGOs (government-oriented NGOs). Democratic power is further diminished as politicians seek legitimacy through the media and corporations. As the welfare state is dismantled, the state retains only an 'enabling role', absenting itself from all but the most minimalist tasks, as reduced levels of welfare are delivered by 'multi-nodal structures' that include state actors (first sector), corporate and business entities (second sector) and NGOs (third sector).[24] Classes, we are constantly told, have vanished as forces of change. Instead, we are free to enter this 'brave new fast-moving porous networked world' as individual consumers of goods and information. We are, in fact, all potential lobbyists for change.[25]

In this way, ideas like the 'public good' and 'public service', and the sense of social solidarity that underpinned the welfare state, have slowly been replaced by the neoliberal ethos of individual responsibility. The removal of safeguards and cultural leeway for ethnic minorities therefore has to be seen in the context of the state absenting itself from a whole range of areas, from protection from the indignities and exploitation of the labour market to defence from floods and climate change. On the one hand, we can take heart from the fact that anger against elected politicians on a multitude of issues (other than immigration) is growing. But we also need to understand that market states and market values persist, with states attempting to resolve the crisis in their legitimacy by reaching towards new models of authoritarianism. Today's reconfigured right is attempting to drive through a new agenda of 'authoritarian collectivism and nationalist compartmentalization',[26] 'hollowing out and destroying' in the process 'the existing sites of democratic possibilities with regard to local authorities and trade unions', and exorcising 'legal and constitutional limits on executive power'.[27] Thanks to the New Right's systematic attack on the 'liberal elite' for its excessive commitment to diversity, a reconfigured right is now free to act as the bold champion of the rights of 'the organic nation' to which we all belong – as long as we leave our 'backward cultures' and regional identities behind. But for those non-citizens who, on account of their 'foreignness' do not belong to the 'organic nation', another set of norms applies.

4

Xeno-Racism and the
Making of 'Enemy Aliens'

In July 2016, snap protests erupted across Australia after ABC broadcast video footage of officials using teargas, spit-hoods and restraints on children, many Aboriginal, held in juvenile detention centres in the Northern Territories. A few weeks later, another scandal was to rock the nation, this time involving the treatment of asylum seekers within Australia's outsourced immigration system. The Nauru files, leaked to the press from a source inside the immigration regime, documented over 2,000 incidents of sexual abuse, self-harm and child abuse, as well as the appalling living conditions at the Nauru detention centre, Papua New Guinea, children being vastly over-represented in the cases reported. You do not have to cross the globe to find such treatment: the same violence has been structured into the private security–dominated systems that Europe has created for refugees and now, by extension, 'enemy aliens'. States, governing at a distance, no longer have a monopoly on force; that, too, has been outsourced. In *A Suitable Enemy*, I described the creation of a separate quasi-penal system for asylum seekers in the context of the new non-colour-coded racism, which treats desperate people as though they were enemies to be corralled into detention centres and, if released, quarantined within an alternative welfare system. But since the book's publication in

2009, the figure of the foreign criminal has emerged in populist folklore as another archetypal cultural bogeyman. Most often dark-skinned, and always racialised, he is predatory and hyper-sexualised or, particularly if she is a Roma, a destitute 'scrounger'. The essentialised and culturally determined deviant nature of the foreign criminal is used to justify the deportation drive against migrants and asylum seekers, the foreign poor and other 'troublesome elements'.

And so it is that ever more categories of people find themselves singled out for deportation, despite having previously enjoyed residence rights. At one end of the spectrum are those convicted of administrative offences relating to immigration, or a number of new criminal offences, such as 'obliging children to beg' (a measure aimed at legitimising the deportation of 'indigenous' EU nationals like the Roma). At the other end are dual nationals and naturalised citizens stripped of their nationality, made vulnerable to deportation and torture when they come under suspicion of terror offences, like Ali Aarrass (see Introduction). But in between are 'virtual nationals', burdened by an existential precariousness that can end in banishment. These are young people, including refugees, who have spent their formative years in Europe (they may even have been born there), but, following a criminal conviction, are marked out as no-hopers to be expelled.[1] Ejected like so much waste, they are transported to a country they have few (or no) connections with, given that they have grown up and been socialised in Europe. In many European countries, it is the norm now that a prison sentence of more than one year renders you deportable.

There is now not only a separate detention regime for asylum seekers and immigration offenders, but also special prison regimes for foreign-national offenders – both underpinned by the introduction of separate principles for foreigners within the legal system.[2] Today, foreign prisoners make up over 30 per cent of the prison population in ten member-states, including Norway, Spain, Belgium and Italy, and over 50 per cent in five, including Austria and small countries with high foreign populations, such as Andorra and Monaco.[3] Thus, a subpopulation of 'deportable subjects' resides within Europe's prison systems. It is the deportation order, not the nature of the offence, that marks prisoners out as permanently dangerous and 'high-risk'; thus, any attempt by the individual to 'reform' seldom makes a difference to their fate.

Double Punishment and Enemy Penology

As 'penal power' is afforded a 'central role in the governance of global migration', criminal justice systems are recalibrated around the xeno-racist policy of 'double punishment' (prison followed by the secondary punishment of deportation).[4] In the past, legal challenges to double punishment in the European Court of Human Rights were treated with care – and politicians acted with caution. It was only in 2003 that Nicolas Sarkozy, as France's interior minister, approved a reform to the penal code to abolish double punishment, on the grounds that 'someone who has spent his childhood in France or has founded a family here should not be subjected to a second penalty'. But by the mid 2000s, as social policy was reshaped around assimilationist (as opposed to integrationist) principles, and cultural–religious explanations for economic and social marginalisation became dominant, politicians sought to contest elections on the issue of 'foreigner crime'. This did not just win them votes; it enabled them to challenge previous legal rulings against double punishment, particularly in cases involving young people. Acting tactically, and bowing to what is termed 'penal populism', politicians of both left and right ensured that resources were directed towards strengthening the infrastructure for the warehousing, disposal and disappearance (by deportation) of surplus 'offending' populations. In the process, the principle of prison as rehabilitation was jettisoned, for the prisoner of migrant origin at least. In true neoliberal fashion, access to packages designed to educate, train and rehabilitate are limited – in preparation for a final abandonment of these prisoners. If prisoners are to be deported at the end of a sentence, prison no longer needs to offer a 'second chance'.

Of course, the law has long held out the possibility of deportation for serious offences; that is not contested. But deportation, even for serious offences, was discretionary (as opposed to automatic) in most of Europe until the first decade of the twenty-first century, and judges would weigh up the justice of deportation against other factors (age, length of residence, family and other ties, compassionate circumstances), using legal principles of proportionality. Now the balance has shifted firmly in favour of deportation for an ever-increasing number of less serious offences, such as criminal damage, low-level drug offences, fights and minor assaults, and non-domestic burglary – offences common among adolescent boys. In the Netherlands, for instance, a law introduced in 2002 allows for the deportation of foreign residents who have been sentenced to one month in prison or one month's community work. (Youngsters whose origins lie in Morocco or the Dutch Caribbean are particularly hard hit.) And new categories of deportable subjects have been created, such as 'prohibited immigrants' in Cyprus, or those with 'special immigration status' in the UK, who live in limbo, temporarily protected from deportation by international law but ultimately liable to expulsion.

In their study of foreign national prisoners in British prisons and immigration removal centres, Turnbull and Hasselberg show that, once you are branded a deportee and therefore unworthy of rehabilitation, you inevitably end up incarcerated in discriminatory prison systems designed to warehouse you prior to deportation. Foreign nationals in the UK have fewer rights than other prisoners, experiencing segregation and more restrictive prison conditions, an inability to access legal rights, longer sentences (including an extra indeterminate period of administrative detention pending deportation); they are, as a consequence, more vulnerable to suicide and self-harm. The Legal Action Group pointed out in its handbook *Foreign*

National Prisoners: Law and Practice that such discrimination violates 'the cardinal principle of the rule of law, equality before the law, prohibiting differentiation between immigrants and British nationals in *areas irrelevant to expulsion*'.[5]

And as with so many government initiatives built on racial exclusion, legal theorists and criminologists have emerged to sugar-coat the policy with constitutional and political theory. Foremost among these is the Hamburg-based criminologist Günther Jakobs, who has developed what Susanne Krasmann has described as an 'enemy penology' – one which has distinct echoes of the work of Carl Schmitt.[6] In 1985, Jakobs identified the need to develop a separate 'criminal law for enemies' (*Feindstrafrecht*). Notorious delinquents, since they were incorrigible, had 'forfeited their status as citizens', and should be denied normal legal guarantees and be combated and excluded, since they represented a fundamental threat to society. His work was based on the idea of a fundamental divide between citizens (subject to the rule of law) and non-citizens (not legal subjects, and therefore non-persons in the eyes of the law). It was subsequently taken up by Otto Depenheuer, chair of constitutional law and legal philosophy at the University of Cologne, but this time in terms of the debate about torture in the context of the fight against Islamic terrorism.[7] In *Selbstbehauptung des Rechtstaates* ('Self-Assertion of the Rule of Law'), Depenheuer claimed that whoever opposed the state and its legal system was an 'enemy *hors de la loi*' (an outlaw). When it was published in 2007, former interior minister and current finance minister Wolfgang Schäuble recommended it as an inspiration and his own bedtime reading.[8]

Jakobs's and Depenheuer's dichotomies – citizens versus non-citizens, enemies versus friends – are increasingly being institutionalised within law, social policy, policing and data collection. They are inherent within racial profiling, both on the streets and in the way information is stored on criminal databases. For example, the Skåne police's *Kringresande* ('itinerants') database, finally deemed unlawful in 2013, comprised a genealogical tree tracing the social and family relations of over 4,029 Roma in Sweden (some of whom had actually died), around 1,000 of whom were children, some as young as two years old. (In June 2016, eight adults and three children whose personal details had been stored in the database were awarded damages for ethnic discrimination in an action brought by Civil Rights Defenders.) Taken as a whole, what we have witnessed across Europe, over at least the last two decades, has been the foregrounding within immigration policies of principles of surveillance and punishment. The less punitive strands of immigration policy, such as civil rights, family reunification and integration, are increasingly only available to the chosen (highly skilled and wealthy) few.

It is not just that there is a two-tier system; it reflects and indeed reinforces the idea that there are effectively now two sets of people: (bad) aliens and (good) immigrants. Stitched into immigration law, in ways that are largely invisible, is 'aliens' law', which invokes a 'hostile environment' forcing undocumented (bad) migrants to live at the margins of society, completely without rights. In the UK in 2013, the Home Office (under then home secretary Theresa May) officially announced its intention to create such a 'hostile environment' for irregular immigrants, sending out vans across London with an advertising board, illustrated with an image of handcuffs, stating 'In the UK illegally? Go home or face arrest.' In 2016, unauthorised working was made a criminal offence, and provisions introduced to confiscate wages as 'proceeds of crime'. Private landlords have been recruited as immigration officers, and the Driver and Vehicle Licensing Agency and banks must check immigration status before issuing driving licences and opening bank accounts.

The parameters of policies aimed at 'aliens' are set in the stone of social control. Immigrants can enjoy pathways to citizenship; but aliens, at every identity check or internal control, carry the border within them. Historically, aliens' laws have reduced residency to a gesture of clemency, a temporary order of hospitality, rescindable at any point. The alternative history has been one of the integration of migrants through immigration policy, whereby they can access social rights, including social care for troubled youngsters at risk of marginality and crime. But now, switching the approach to treat juveniles from a migrant background as aliens ensures that those who 'fall through the net' and commit crimes will never be allowed to integrate. Punitive policies aimed at those deemed alien means that resources that were formerly allocated to social care, anti-discrimination and integration can be transferred into immigration enforcement, punishment, warehousing and banishment.

Electoral Politics and Racialised Insecurities

These policy and legal changes did not occur in a vacuum, but were linked to the media's fascination with 'foreigner crime' and the threading of media frameworks into political rhetoric. At the end of the 1990s, right-wing media outlets and centre-right politicians were pushing far more aggressively at the 'foreigner crime' issue, particularly in local and regional elections. In the United States, the criminologist Jonathan Simon, in *Governing through Crime*, demonstrated how crime had earlier become central to the exercise of authority, regional executives and city mayors defining their objectives in prosecutorial terms and framing political issues in language shaped by public insecurity and outrage about crimes that were more often than not racialised.[9] Exactly the same process has now happened in Europe.

Sensationalising crime has, of course, been the way to sell newspapers from time immemorial. But just as nativism ('our own people first') has become the norm at a time of a shrinking welfare state and growing joblessness, the fear of crime has come to the fore amid the mass insecurity provoked by globalisation. Sections of the media can now be relied upon to pander to xenophobia, conjuring up the vices of the 'outsider' and the virtues of the 'insider', appealing in particular to the machismo of white heterosexual men in the face of the alien threat posed to 'our women'. Indeed, the xenophobic populism promoted in the media seems to be designed to appeal to the worst instincts of the nativist imagination – a veritable well of repressed racial feeling and angst that can also be tapped by the extreme right, and is indeed the mainstay today of Breitbart News London and other new far-right media outlets such as the AltRight Corporation, a news site backed by the US white supremacist Richard Spencer in partnership with the Swedish publishing house Arktos Media and Red Ice, a Swedish-based video and podcast platform.

In the post–Second World War period, the forcible repatriation of second- and third-generation 'migrant' youth was only a campaign objective of the far right and neo-Nazi fringe. The first intimations that such policies were becoming normalised came in a referendum on immigrant crime in Switzerland in 1997: in the general election, the nativist right-wing populist Swiss People's Party (SVP) campaigned for a referendum on introducing measures to allow for the deportation of the entire family of a convicted criminal under the age of eighteen. Subsequently, in the general election campaign, the SVP issued a crude and blatantly racist poster that showed three white sheep kicking a black sheep against a backdrop of the Swiss flag. In state elections in Germany in 1998, the Christian Social Union (CSU) administration in Bavaria made foreigner crime its central electoral issue, despite the fact that Bavaria had one of the lowest crime rates in the whole of Germany. The call by Interior Minister Günther Beckstein for the deportation of entire immigrant families in cases where under-age members were found guilty of offences, even if the offenders or their parents were born in Germany, had particularly nasty undertones, given that it had been the Nazis who first introduced the principle of *Sippenhaft* ('kin liability'). In fact, the German centre-right drew on the campaign tactics deployed by the SVP in Switzerland. Thus, the mainstream has travelled firmly into the 'send them back' territory of the extreme right.

In the Bavarian case, the CSU had been looking to build its

election campaign around the threat posed by 'juvenile delinquents' from a 'migrant background', and the case of 'Mehmet'
provided the opening. It was journalists on newspapers like
Bild that made the running for the politicians, turning the
abstract issue of 'foreigner crime' into a concrete cause by
publicising the case of thirteen-year-old 'Mehmet', the 'terror
kid' with sixty-two criminal offences to his name.[10] As a child,
this youngster would have been protected by data protection laws from naming and shaming in the media – hence the
pseudonym 'Mehmet' was chosen to describe the incorrigible
'criminal monster' who had to be deported to ensure the safety
of the public. Not everyone was impressed by the monstering
of Mehmet. Ekkehard Müller-Jentsch, editor of *Süddeutsche
Zeitung*, criticised the CSU decision to make the teenager an
example, saying the campaign was never about how to address
juvenile offending rates, but was instead based on an opportunistic desire to trawl for the perfect case to serve political
and commercial media interests. As a result of the political and
media offensive, in 1998 'Mehmet' became the first teenager to
be deported from Germany, although he was returned in 2002
after the Federal Administrative Court ruled the deportation
unlawful. On the eve of his return, the symbiosis of the politics of *Bild* and the needs of the CSU was evident. *Bild* carried
the headline 'Please, Spare Us, Mehmet', while interior minister
Beckstein reiterated that Muhlis Ari (as he was now officially
known) would always remain a foreigner.

Enemy penology continued to shape the debate about juvenile delinquency in Germany, with the CDU's Hesse governor
Roland Koch calling in 2008 for the deportation of foreign
youths sentenced to one year or more in prison, and *Bild* once
again lending strong editorial support to Koch's campaign.
Chancellor Merkel's claim, on the basis of dubious crime statistics, that 43 percent of all violent crimes in Germany were
committed by people under twenty-one, almost half of whom
were from an immigrant background, led to the *Bild* headline:
'Young Foreigners More Violent than Young Germans', and

almost daily news stories about 'foreign' repeat offenders with long criminal records.

When the Media Turns Prosecutor

In May 1999, in the small village of Kollum, in the largely rural province of Friesland in the Netherlands, a sixteen-year-old local girl called Marianne Vaatstra was raped and murdered, her throat cut as she cycled home from a disco in the early hours of the morning. What happened next can only be described as a witch-hunt against asylum seekers living at the Poelpleats temporary reception centre (AZC). Suspicion had fallen on the residents of Poelpleats. Rumours circulated locally that the police had failed to investigate AZC residents, allowing an Iraqi suspect to disappear without trace. From May onwards, Kollum began to dominate media stories, particularly after 8 October, when a riot erupted at a consultation meeting in the village about building a permanent asylum residence, the AZC and the Vaatstra case emerging as the main item of discussion on national radio, and TV crews inundating the village.

The police's supposed failings and politically correct attitudes towards the asylum seekers became the refrain in much media debate. But crime reporter Peter R. de Vries, who hosted a popular national crime-watch programme, took the hysteria to new heights by legitimising on TV the rumours against the AZC. Even after the Iraqi suspect was tracked down in Istanbul and it was established through DNA samples that he was not the murderer, de Vries continued to suggest that the police had been involved in a conspiracy to cover up the fact that asylum seekers were suspected of the crime, because the government feared loss of support for their policy of dispersing asylum seekers around the country. By this time, the police investigation was being seriously hampered by the media hysteria that surrounded the case. The police pointed out that, of 500 tip-offs received from the public, and of 1,000 statements taken as a result of these tip-offs, not one mentioned a dark-skinned person near the scene of the crime.

To this day, the Dutch still use terminology like 'non-Western immigrants' or *allochtoon* ('non-native') when discussing race relations. Such terminology helps to explain the durability of racist frameworks in its media, and the critical role the media has played in shaping criminal justice policies to enable a lower deportation threshold. As far back as 1999, sections of the media had gone in hot pursuit of the dangerous and primitive *allochtoon*. They went even further than *Bild*, in that they substituted themselves for the police and the prosecution service in a criminal investigation. The case of Marianne Vaatstra turned out to be a pivotal moment in the reshaping of the Dutch criminal justice system towards a greater reliance on deportation.

For sixteen years, the myth persisted that the police were involved in a conspiracy to cover up the identity of the perpetrators. Then, in 2016, on the basis of new DNA evidence, a Dutch farmer from a nearby village was arrested for the teenager's killing. But nothing could undo the damage done in 1999–2000. The press treatment of the Marianne Vaatstra case over a six-month period had furthered the cause of racism in the Netherlands. During the witch-hunt, the Dutch campaigner Mieke Hoppe and I criticised the frameworks of the media. For so doing, we were bombarded with complaints and accused of labelling all the villagers of Kollum as racists (which we had not). A local anti-discrimination body publicly distanced itself from our critique, even before reading it. (They later sent us some Friesland cheese – a speciality of the region – by way of apology.)[11]

Scaremongering media frameworks based on racialised police crime statistics are still a cause for deep concern, as is the discriminatory nature of 'criminal perpetrator' databases that gather information on *allochtoons* on the grounds of ethnicity, thereby treating young people whose family origins are in Morocco or the Dutch Caribbean as potential criminals, and hence deportable subjects. So, for example, the Dutch data protection agency, with the housing ministry, operated a database on 'problematic youth', the Reference Index of Antilleans, which registered information on young people on the grounds of ethnicity, thereby treating every Antillean child as a potential criminal. The database was declared unlawful in a 2009 legal challenge by the Dutch Caribbean Consultative Body and the Open Society Justice Initiative.

Likewise, in Italy, laws allowing for the deportation of a greater array of foreigners were introduced in 2007, following saturation media coverage of immigrant crime that reached such proportions in the spring and summer of 2007 that the UN High Commissioner for Refugees intervened. He warned that the media were acting as a sounding board for the worst manifestations of hate, and called on editors-in-chief to desist from using alarmist and combative language. By November of that year, *Guardian* journalist John Hooper was drawing attention to an anti-foreigner climate unparalleled in the post–Second World War years.[12] At the end of October 2007, the Prodi government passed an emergency decree allowing the speedy expulsion of EU nationals, as hate against Romanians escalated following the sexual assault and murder of Giovanna Reggiani, the wife of a navy captain, allegedly by a Romanian Roma man, in Rome. Prime ministerial candidate Silvio Berlusconi built on the hate in the run-up to the 2008 general election, describing jobless foreigners as 'an army of evil', and calling for the establishment of special camps in which they could be interned. In Rome, the newly elected fascist mayor promised to expel from the city 20,000 immigrants who he claimed had been released into the community after serving prison sentences. Later in that year the Berlusconi government passed a law enabling automatic deportation of EU citizens committing crimes carrying a two-year prison sentence – a measure declared unlawful by the European Commissioner and partially rescinded in October 2008.

Anti-Roma scaremongering was behind much of this new legislative agenda, linked as it was to the introduction of the so-called Nomad State of Emergency that followed the murder

of Giovanna Reggiani. At the same time, there had been a proposal for a national census of the Gypsy population living in
the 'nomad camps', which would include the fingerprinting
of all Roma. Though the Council of State ruled the 'Nomad
State of Emergency' unlawful in November 2011, the register of the homeless people living in camps (the inhabitants
of which also include migrants from North Africa and other
refugees), implemented in July 2010, is ongoing (albeit without
the fingerprinting). At the time of writing, there are renewed
fears in Italy that another wave of anti-Romanian sentiment is
about to be unleashed, with far-right parties demanding a new
law on legitimate self-defence following an incident in Gug-
nano, northern Italy, in which a restaurant owner shot dead
a Romanian man who, he says, was part of a gang about to
rob him. Luigi di Maio, the deputy head of the Italian Chamber of Deputies and a member of the Five Star Movement,
claimed on Facebook: 'Italy has imported 40% of Romania's
criminals.'

In recent years, the media's agenda is not so much merely
intertwined with the political and legislative agenda as driving
it. When the media launch a moral panic about foreign criminals, they can do so knowing that their stories can make or
break political careers. An intimation of this power came in
April 2006, when the British Labour home secretary Charles
Clarke was forced to resign four days after the tabloid frenzy
that accompanied the revelation that between 1999 and 2006,
over 1,000 foreign nationals, including some convicted of very
serious crimes, had been released from prison on completion of
their sentences without the required investigation into whether
they should be deported. According to Luke de Noronha, 'certain heinous offences were inordinately covered in the press
and made to represent the "crisis" … journalists and parliamentarians consistently invoke the "rapist" and "murderer" …
The "foreign criminal" is made "foreign" through association with violence (often sexual).'[13] According to de Noronha,
around one-third of articles on 'foreign criminals' featured

the word 'rape' or 'rapist', even though only nine of the 1,023 released offenders had been charged with rape. As a result of the subsequent moral panic, foreign nationals who had been released from prison were rounded up and re-detained, and those about to complete their sentence were told, without any reasons given, that they would not be released. Subsequently, the UK Borders Act 2007 was passed, providing for automatic deportation (subject to human rights law, whereby a real risk of torture or strong family ties could prevent expulsion) of anyone convicted of specific offences or sentenced to at least twelve months' imprisonment in total. Following this, in 2009, the prisons minister introduced a 'hub-and-spoke' policy, whereby certain prisons, defined as 'hub' prisons, were devoted wholly or primarily to the holding of non-citizens ('spoke' prisons also held non-citizens, although fewer). Immigration officials were embedded in the 'hubs' to facilitate deportation processes. Now, even liberal-minded politicians in Europe today are terrified for their careers should they be seen to relax deportation policies and release non-citizen ex-offenders back into the community. In an interview with the *New Statesman* in February 2009, Charles Clarke blamed not just his own sacking but other New Labour decisions on 'chronic fear of the media, especially the Murdoch press'.

Cologne and Liberal Flight

More recently, we have seen a dramatic and rapid capitulation of the liberal media to hard-right, anti-refugee rhetoric in Germany. After a spate of crimes, initially blamed on refugees, at New Year's Eve festivities in Cologne on 31 December 2015, large swathes of the press took fright as social media and the comments pages of national newspapers were inundated by anti-refugee, anti-foreigner opinion – and journalists, now described in far-right terms as *Lügenpresse* ('lying press'), found themselves the target of vitriolic hatred.

To understand the extent of the liberal media's capitulation, one needs to turn the clock back three months, to September 2015 and the publication of Turkish journalist Nilüfer Demir's photograph of the body of Alan Kurdi, a three-year-old Syrian-Kurdish refugee child washed ashore and lying lifeless on a beach near Bodrum. The image was syndicated across the world, provoking a global wave of shock and sympathy and a momentary shift in the political discourse on refugees. Even newspapers like *Bild*, the *Sun* and the *Daily Mail*, so hostile to refugees, took a softer stance. Two days after Alan Kurdi's death, Chancellor Merkel suspended the Dublin regulation and, declaring 'yes we can', allowed Syrian refugees to travel to Germany via a humanitarian corridor from northern Greece to southern Bavaria. The immediate response of ordinary people based on *Gastrecht* ('hospitality') was impressive. Indeed, a poll by the Bertelsmann Foundation suggested that at least one in five Germans (and 44 per cent of German Muslims) had helped refugees. But the right was merely biding its time.

Cologne provided everything it had been looking for – a chance, in the words of Helge Malchow, director of the Kiepenheuer & Witsch publishing house, to transform the prevailing 'welcoming culture' into one based on 'rejection and fear'.[14] Ever since the popularisation at far-right Pegida street rallies of the chant *Lügenpresse!*, social media have been used to whip up anger at journalists accused of political correctness and refusing to 'tell the truth' about Muslims and refugees. Until the events of Cologne, this was the echo-chamber in which Pegida supporters vented their fury at the liberal and left media. But when crimes were committed by gangs of petty criminals – most, allegedly, dark-skinned – at the New Year celebrations in Cologne, the liberal press emerged as easy prey for the extreme right, which instrumentalised the crimes, using them to mock liberals – Alternative for Germany (AfD) described them sarcastically as *Gutmenschen* ('good people') – and force them into a more muscular stance. Some Social Democrat, Green and even Left party politicians now joined the clamour for more deportations, arguing that German taxpayers should not 'pay to imprison foreign criminals' (Sigmar Gabriel, SPD) and that 'whoever abuses the right to hospitality has lost the right to be a guest' (Sahra Wagenknecht, Left Party).

The success of the extreme right's campaign exposed the shallowness of the liberal press's support for child refugees like Alan Kurdi. It was a support based on pity – an emotion that is too often evoked only by the pure, unblemished character of the suffering victim. As Transform Network analysts Walter Baier and Matthias Kötter pointed out, Cologne was a victory for the hard right, which successfully shifted a previously liberal consensus towards a racist, reactionary consensus, the liberal press now joining those who questioned the right to hospitality.[15]

The facts about who exactly committed the crimes at Cologne, especially as only a minority of suspects were ever formally identified, are hard to come by. But if you had been following rumours circulating on social media in early January 2016, you would have been convinced that nearly all the 1,054 criminal offences committed by drunken and petty criminal elements were perpetrated by Syrian refugees.[16] Indeed, the scandal, the real story that should have been brought to the fore, was the minimal police presence at the festivities. As a result of inadequate police numbers, women found themselves hemmed in, cut off from their friends and groped, before having their mobile phones stolen (at least two rapes were also reported).

At no time following the incidents in Cologne has the hard right shown any interest in the facts. The AfD and its intellectual supporters used the crimes to attack Angela Merkel's so-called 'open door' policy. Once again alleging political correctness (a media and police conspiracy to cover up foreigner crime), they began the call for more deportations. Not surprisingly, Merkel's government was quick to assuage public opinion, and a new deportation law was announced. The only positive result was a commitment to change Germany's law on sexual offences. At the time of writing, sexual assault or rape is prosecutable only if a woman can prove that she resisted.[17]

AfD, with strong support from illiberal elements in the media, played a central role in shutting the door on liberal opinion by promoting the idea that, in the wake of the events in Cologne, the media could not be trusted, particularly on stories relating to refugees. Cologne was a 'foretaste of our country's impending cultural and civilisational collapse', claimed the AfD, whose then leader, Frauke Petry, asked Merkel on Facebook: 'Is Germany now open and colourful enough for you, following the waves of crimes and sexual attacks?'

The Limits of Liberalism

Today, the liberal media (and not just in Germany) are quicker than ever to mark out the ethnic background of perpetrators of crime, adopting right-wing frameworks that racialise crime. In Sweden, headlines have become more blunt, one columnist on the *Dagens Nyheter* pointing out: 'If there was an opinion corridor [ie, a range of acceptable public opinions] it has now been thoroughly demolished.'[18] Thomas Meaney believes that the German liberal press is 'rushing to make clear their new vigilance'. He cites Josef Joffe's column in *Die Zeit* warning that '[o]pen borders will close open hearts'.[19]

In *Regarding the Pain of Others*, Susan Sontag points out that photography has always been 'at the service of consumerist manipulations', and that exploitation of sentiments such as pity is also a 'source of value'. But so too is the sentiment of fear, for 'the more diffuse and spectre-like the threat at the border, the higher the potential gains from the phantom menace'.[20] The tiny body of Alan Kurdi once evoked feelings of pity, but after the events in Cologne, the notorious satirical French magazine *Charlie Hebdo* sought to turn pity into disgust. Under the caption 'What Would Little Aylan Be Like if He Had Lived?', the cartoonist 'Riss' depicted animal-like migrants running after women, attempting to pinch their bottoms.[21] In Germany, too, racist and Orientalist images were published in response

91

to Cologne, in the nominally liberal *Süddeutsche Zeitung* and the more conservative *Focus*. *Süddeutsche Zeitung*'s cartoon featured black hands groping a white woman's crotch, and appeared alongside an article in which a psychologist claimed that, for all young Muslim men, every meeting with a woman was a highly sexualised encounter. *Focus*, meanwhile, was even more graphic, publishing a photograph of a naked white woman with black handprints on her body. Editor-in-chief Ulrich Reitz said that anyone who called it racist was 'afraid of the truth'.[22]

Moral panics over foreigner crime serve multiple purposes. The manipulation of fear serves as an accelerator for penal power and militarisation and, in this project, the archetype of the dangerous, sexually predatory, marauding male migrant is central. It is a smokescreen behind which the rich North hides the fact that it has abandoned refugees and migrants to the free market. Strategies of abandonment and state-sanctioned harm and violence, including cruel and degrading treatment and torture, go hand in hand. The media talk of the violence of 'foreign criminals', but seldom the violence of the state. And as the potential grows for a reconfigured hard right to capture state power in a fractious EU with a diminished human rights framework, the racism and authoritarianism of the state emerges as the burning issue of our times and the key site of struggle.

III.

Fallout

5

The EU, Uneven Development, and the Nationalist Backlash

In January 2017, in the northern city of Amiens, in a region that has France's highest rate of unemployment, the US manu-facturer of household appliances Whirlpool announced that, by June 2018, its local plant producing tumble dryers would close. Three hundred workers would be affected by the company's decision to relocate to Poland, where labour is cheaper. A strike committee was quickly formed, and pickets organised outside the factory. Then, on 26 April, only three days after the first-round of the presidential election, the media descended on the city. Amiens is the home town of Emmanuel Macron, the former Rothschild investment banker whose 'centrist' presidential bid had been carefully crafted by big business and the media.[1] On that day, Macron was due to meet union representatives from Whirlpool at the chamber of commerce a few miles from the plant. Enter, stage-left, Marine Le Pen, the so-called people's candidate for president, in town to upstage Macron, speak out for workers and join the picket line. To whistles and calls of 'Marine for president!', she turned to the microphones, attack-ing Macron as being 'with the oligarchs, with the employers'. As the storm clouds gather over a Europe where old right-wing political elites feel under threat from their ultra-nationalist flank, the neoliberal state – as the rise of brand Macron suggests – is attempting to reassert its authority and resolve its dispute with nationalist elites, albeit in novel ways.

Nationalist and nativist politics are playing out across the EU at a time of economic retrenchment as well as austerity – an accelerated form of the neoliberal project of globalising financial markets, shrinking welfare, deregulating labour and privatising state assets. When public services are being decimated and jobs are haemorrhaging, particularly in the former industrial heartlands, it is not hard to see why demands for economic protectionism are popular. Nor can the ultra-nationalists' criticisms of the EU – a supranational polity driven by corporate interests and controlled by an 'unelected' and 'unaccountable' European Commission – be dismissed out of hand.[2] Political parties have much to lose if they uncritically support the status quo, or too openly parade their allegiance to global capital, as shown by the decline in support (and membership) of traditional centre-left and centre-right parties. To get an idea of the humiliation currently inflicted by the electorate on mainstream social liberal parties, just turn to the French presidential elections, where the Socialist candidate, Benoît Hamon, came in fourth, with just 6.36 per cent of the vote. National elections in Europe are increasingly proving inconclusive, two-party systems are giving way to multi-party systems, and coalition governments often take months to form. As the political centre of European politics is transformed, anti-immigrant, Eurosceptic and nativist parties, as well as the old extreme right, are advancing. But so too are social movements, environmental parties, and an anti-austerity left – moving, admittedly in fits and starts, but creating new frameworks, sowing the seeds of progress, and courageously opening up spaces for struggle.

Whether the reconfiguring hard right – fortified by the ultra-nationalist rebellion within mainstream conservatism – represents neoliberalism's nemesis or its resolution, is by no means clear. But nationalism and neoliberalism are already combining in ways that suggest that, in the short term at least, the centre of political culture in many of the EU's member-states will take a more illiberal turn, and not just in response to immigration. The impact of nationalism on the state, state racism and the relations between labour and capital is the subject of this chapter. Nationalism, racism and the right have to be discussed in the context of uneven development within the EU, and the core–periphery relationship that has solidified within the Eurozone, where Germany is without doubt hegemonic. A discussion of the differences and similarities between the solutions offered by the nationalists, whether in Europe's east, north, south or west, throws light on its political direction, as well as on the kind of state power that is emerging in different regions.

Post-Communism and Failed Transition

In April 2017, a fascinating article in the *London Review of Books* began by examining the loss in 2007 of 500 jobs at Cadbury's Somerdale chocolate factory near Bristol, which was relocating to Skarbimierz, Poland. Its author, James Meek, questions how Poland, a beneficiary of €130 billion in EU investment in roads, railways and schools, could, in 2015, have elected the hard-line Catholic fundamentalist, authoritarian, populist, Eurosceptic Law and Justice Party (PiS).[3] Part of the answer lies in the free-market economic shock therapy that accompanied its entry into the EU, wiping out state manufacturing and privatising state assets only to deliver temporary jobs, temporary factories and special zones where foreign companies would pay no taxes for ten years, and 50 per cent tax for the ten years after that. Integration into the EU came in 2004 for the Visegrád countries (the Czech Republic, Hungary, Poland and Slovakia), Estonia, Latvia, Lithuania and Slovenia, 2007 for Bulgaria and Romania, and 2013 for Croatia. But the transition from a command economy to a market economy failed by any criteria. At first, governing elites embraced neoliberalism wholeheartedly:

the pursuit of wealth, which would trickle down as long as everyone embraced capitalism and acted out of self-interest, was invested with a quasi-religious value. But since the financial crash of 2008, it has become blindingly obvious that wealth, far from trickling down, is cascading upwards. Research into male mortality rates in the post-communist countries of eastern Europe and the Soviet Union, published in the *Lancet* in 2009, found that the social stress engendered by mass privatisation had led to a 12.8 percent increase in male deaths from 1989 to 2002.[4] Furthermore, in 2012, a study by Harvard and Cambridge economists published in the *American Sociological Review* found a direct link between the mass fiscal shock caused by privatisation programmes in many former communist countries and the economic failure and corruption that followed.[5] The mandatory privatisation of public pension schemes proved another comprehensive disaster for the countries involved, leading to extremes of pensioner poverty.

In the post-communist states of the EU, neoliberal market reforms were imposed in the name of democratisation. Here, parties of the authoritarian right are advancing, taking advantage of a 'broader rebellion against the outcomes of the "transition process" that was implemented after the collapse of Communist Party rule'.[6] The Hungarian Civic Union (Fidesz) was elected for a second term in Hungary in 2014, while in Poland, in 2015, PiS swept away Civic Platform (PO), the party previously headed by Donald Tusk (now president of the European Council). PiS, previously a neoliberal party, successfully fought the autumn 2015 election on a programme of economic protection. Its success owes much to dislike of the PO, which under Tusk's leadership held the poor and the vulnerable in disdain. In Slovakia, fourteen neo-fascists from People's Party – Our Slovakia (L'SNS), headed by Marián Kotleba, governor of the Banská Bystrica region, entered parliament for the first time in May 2016, a fact that owed a great deal to the space opened up by the divisive politics of the (nominally) social-democratic Direction – Social Democracy (Smer-SD), under the leadership of Robert Fico. Having lost its majority in the 2016 general election, Smer-SD currently heads a weak four-party coalition government.

Neoliberalism, with its promise of abundant riches and freedom, no longer provides a plausible script, particularly as systemic corruption is becoming institutionalised within the political process. Hence the comfort of the sticking-plaster of nationalism, and the narratives of anti-multiculturalism and anti-immigration. Mainstream politicians in Hungary, Poland and Slovakia speak the tired old language of authoritarianism, ethnic nationalism and the nation-state, with nineteenth-century-style social Darwinism and anti-Roma and anti-migrant racism providing pitch and tenor. The disciplinary power of religion – Catholicism or Calvinism – is also invoked to maintain social control in the face of the narcissistic lifestyles of the super-rich. In Hungary, Fidesz has resurrected the notion of the 'Christian-national idea' – a reference, whether conscious or unconscious, to the dominant state ideology of the Horthy era, when the word 'Christian' was used to denote someone who was 'not Jewish' and to limit Jewish participation in public life. Orbán's conflation today of Christian and national themes has hitched Christianity to the nativist cause (internationalism and compassion towards non-natives, according to Orbán, are forms of political correctness), while introducing the 'workfare society'. 'Family', 'work', 'order', 'nation' – the values written into the new Hungarian Constitution – provide the framework for 'workfare' in the form of the compulsory Hungarian Work Plan (HWP). This is the kind of punitive programme that Donald Trump would be proud of. It is based on hard labour in forestry, waterworks and local renovation, where so-called 'jobs' have been divested of the normal rights associated with labour. Not surprisingly, the HWP only came into being on the back of the racialisation of poverty – including constant attacks on the 'indolent' and undisciplined Roma.

But old-style authoritarianism is hitched to modern forms of mass surveillance, exemplified by the detailed system of media-content regulation (including internet and social media content) introduced in Hungary. And there is still good old-fashioned state control of the media (as well as censorship) to rely on. In Hungary, a proposed amendment to the National Security Act that would have allowed state intelligence agents to be stationed inside newsrooms was narrowly avoided in June 2015, after protests forced its withdrawal. In Poland a new law allowing government control of the state media was justified on grounds that 'public media are ignoring their mission towards the nation'.[7]

Right-wing Poland and Hungary, just like Spain (see below), are engaging in 'memory wars'. These are a continuation of the New Right's culture wars, but this time on the battlefield of memory, attempting to establish a puerile reading of historical events that highlights patriotism, heroism and sacrifice throughout history.[8] Hungarian memory wars centre on the construction of a national memorial portraying Hungary as the victim of the German occupation of 1944, the erection of statues that celebrate anti-Semitic politicians associated with the Horthy era (1919–44), and laws criminalising the insulting or demeaning of national symbols, all backed up by a nationalist school curriculum and attacks on educational institutions such as the Central European University and the Georg Lukács Archives in Budapest. In addition, the Veritas Institute ('Institute of Truth'), staffed by revisionist and right-wing historians who downplay the participation of Hungarians in the murder of 500,000 Hungarian Jews during the Second World War, enjoys the patronage of the Fidesz government. In Poland the factual underpinnings of post–Second World War history are also undergoing reconstruction, the role played by the Solidarity trades union and its leader Lech Wałęsa – now derided by the right as a traitor – in securing the transition through negotiations with the Communist Party now being hotly disputed. For the PiS and the far-right parties, the real patriots were the 'cursed soldiers', those who resisted the imposition of Soviet communism in the 1940s through guerrilla warfare and personal sacrifice. In line with this glorious history of military resistance have come attempts to criminalise those who seek to explore issues of collaboration with the Holocaust following the German invasion in 1939. The state took particular exception to Pawel Pawlikowski's Oscar-winning 2014 film *Ida*, which tells the story of a young novitiate nun who, on learning that she was born Jewish, returns to the grave of her murdered parents. Law and Justice has drafted a law that seeks to punish with a fine or imprisonment anyone who, intentionally or inadvertently, ascribes responsibility to the Polish nation or state 'for crimes committed by the German Third Reich'.

Today's post-communist nationalist leaders launch witch-hunts for internal and external enemies, conjuring up new threats in the face of every attempt to expose their corruption and perversion of power. The War on Terror and the EU's disastrous handling of the refugee crisis have provided ammunition for the likes of Viktor Orbán (Fidesz), Jaroslaw Kaczyński (Law and Justice) and Robert Fico (Smer-DS) to attack the EU, which is said to be imposing immigration, multiculturalism, gender and gay rights on culturally homogeneous and socially conservative societies. Orbán and Kaczyński, as well as the Czech president Miloš Zeman, all openly speak in crude terms about racial and cultural survival, 'vital instincts' and 'everyday patriotism'. Like Fico, Zeman, who has addressed anti-Islam rallies organised by the far right, is nominally a Social Democrat. None of these parties is averse to stoking anti-German sentiment. Merkel, for instance, has been portrayed in the Polish state-controlled media either in Nazi uniform or as a nineteenth-century-style imperialist dismembering the nation, while Orbán has raged against Germany's 'moral imperialism'.[9]

These new (and sometimes not so new) corrupt elites, in countries with little experience of modern immigration, are manipulating a victim narrative, issuing dire warnings about foreign domination while covering up their own failure to protect their people from the ravages of neoliberalism. Entry into the EU meant that manufacturing industries, once the pride of the Soviet bloc, were now deemed uncompetitive, and condemned to wither on the vine. State assets, including the banks, were privatised. Today's banks in east and central Europe are between 60 and 90 per cent cent foreign-owned, Austrian, German French and Italian banks being the biggest winners. The 2008 economic crisis delivered another blow. Foreign banks threatened to pull out or scale back to maintain their liquidity in home countries, leading to EU- and IMF-imposed austerity in Hungary, Romania and Latvia.

First in Hungary, and now in Poland, the ingredients of a liberal democracy that were necessary for EU entry, such as an independent media and judiciary and adherence to the constitution, have been or are being dismantled, to the embarrassment of the European Commission. (Once in the EU, it is legally impossible to be kicked out – though, in theory, a state may be stripped of its voting rights.) Hungary – once the 'happiest barracks in the Soviet camp' – provides one of the most dramatic examples of a 'post-Communist mafia state', defined by the former liberal education minister, Bálint Magyar, as a new type of state power, a 'sub-set of autocracy', spinning around a 'centralised monopoly of corruption' in an 'organised upperworld'.[10]

Poland, capitalism's post-communist poster child, attempts to fast-track the implementation of the constitutional and administrative changes already made in Hungary. The financialised corruption in the wealthier core EU countries, which enriches multinationals and turns a blind eye to tax evasion, has its counterpart in Hungary in bribe-taking and systemic corruption within the political class.

The immiseration of these countries is evidenced by the fact that today the most active and skilled members of their labour forces work abroad, mostly in western Europe – where, despite EU membership, they are afforded a second-class status. Former Conservative British prime minister David Cameron's poisonous language about EU migrant workers 'demanding something for nothing' and his pre-Brexit negotiations to secure an 'emergency brake' mechanism to make payment of in-work benefits to Europeans conditional on their having worked in Britain for at least eighteen months, have cemented and legitimated this second-class status. Cameron's attempts to appear tough on free movement were based on misleading calculations made by the Department for Work and Pensions, and subsequently released to the *Times*, which claimed that 40 per cent of recent EU migrants (148,000) claimed in-work benefits. After questioning HMRC, the *Guardian* ascertained that the total figure was 84,000 over a period of four years. Moreover, as the tax office considers any family with an EU partner to be an EU migrant family, even when the other partner is British, many British nationals and their children appear to be classified as 'migrant families'.[11]

National Elites Challenged in Austria and Germany

By 2014, Pegida was causing havoc in Dresden and other cities in eastern Germany, raging against Muslims and immigrants and mobilising tens of thousands of people on the street. But Pegida was not the only problem facing the mainstream right. The Christian Democrats faced a rebellion in their own ranks, some of their members being among the founders of Alternative for Germany (AfD). Seemingly a more moderate threat than Pegida, the AfD was initially formed as a Eurosceptic party, and dubbed the 'party of the professors'. Merkel, then, not only faced rebellion from within her own ranks, but the risk of right-wing contagion from eastern Europe, with a mix of autarky, nationalism, corruption and racism threatening to contaminate politics in eastern Germany. There are certain cities and regions at the EU's core, in Austria and eastern Germany, that are experiencing a mix of economic stagnation, low birth rates and depopulation. Much of the former GDR – particularly Thuringia and Saxony, where the Islamophobic street movement Pegida is rooted and AfD has its strongest base – is nostalgic for the certainties of the communist era. (There is even a name for it: *Ostalgie*.) Meanwhile, in Austria, the dominance of the two main parties – centre-right and centre-left – within a social-partnership governance framework is no longer guaranteed. For the first time since 1945, the candidates of the Social Democrats and centre-right People's Party failed to make it to the second round of the 2016 presidential elections. More shockingly, the extreme-right Freedom Party's Norbert Hofer (who claims to carry a gun to 'protect him from refugees') won the first round, taking 35 per cent of the vote. Hofer was narrowly defeated in the second round by the independent candidate Alexander van der Bellen, but a re-run was called due to alleged electoral irregularities. Although Hofer lost fairly decisively in the December 2016 re-run, the Freedom Party (FPÖ) had managed to shift the debate on immigration even further to the right, as evidenced in the passage of a new asylum law (mirroring a law already passed in Hungary) allowing the government to introduce a state of emergency at a time of migration crisis.

The roots of the Freedom Party (FPÖ) lie in Austria's fascist past: its first leader, Anton Reinthaller, was a member of the Nazi SS who served as agriculture minister after Hitler's annexation of Austria in 1938. In recent years it has extended its power base from the deep rural southern state of Carinthia to the working-class, formerly Social Democrat strongholds in Vienna and Lower Austria – as well as, crucially, the eastern border states of Styria and Burgenland. In the latter state, in 2015, the local branch of the Social Democrats, to its everlasting shame, formed a coalition government with the FPÖ. At the time of writing, the attitude of the Social Democratic Party as a whole to the question of further power-sharing with the FPÖ, whether regional or national, has yet to be resolved.

Meanwhile, back in Germany, Chancellor Merkel was by 2013 facing strong pressure from within the Christian Democrats to accommodate to the arguments of Pegida. But she quickly imposed her will, pointing to the threat of Russian influence within Pegida's ranks. This also explains her carefully crafted constitutional response to Donald Trump's election in the United States. She was looking forward to working with Trump, she said, on the basis of 'shared values of democracy, freedom and respect for the law and the dignity of man, independent of origin, skin colour, religion, gender, sexual orientation or political views'.

But Merkel's stance has also to be related back to the wider splits in national conservatism, particularly over the Greek debt crisis and the Eurozone. In 2013, Germany's Christian Democrats were divided primarily over this question.[12] In the post-war period, Germany gained a reputation as the European country least prone to nationalist rhetoric, and one that consciously sought to refashion its identity within Europe. Until 2013, Europhilia and support for globalisation held the line, reflecting too the importance of the EU and global markets (most recently Latin America and Asia) to Germany's export-oriented economy and its successful multinationals. Now Merkel faced not only AfD, a Eurosceptic party exploiting discontent about Germany's future role in the Eurozone, but also a xenophobic media campaign supportive of AfD positions, and openly attacking the 'greedy' and 'lazy' Greeks. Thus, discontent came from within centre-right circles, where a major argument had been brewing over supposed economic laxity in the context of the global financial crisis, and in particular the debt crisis in Greece.

In this way, the global banking crisis of 2008 threw up contradictions within the centre-right over ordoliberalism, the German economic orthodoxy holding that government actions should be subordinated to the strict observance of an established order, with the function of a strong state being to 'consciously shape the structures, the institutional framework, the order, in which the economy functions'.[13] Germany's 'social market economy' (the state regulates, but does not stimulate) has always rejected Keynesian solutions in a recession, as has the European Central Bank, which Germany has fashioned in its own image. At first, there was no open rift between political parties about Germany's future in the Eurozone. But German and French banks had lent billions to Greece (and more to Spain), which put them at risk – and this exposure was represented in the media not as a crisis of the banks, but as a crisis of debt in the southern European periphery caused by an excess of public spending. Germany, with its strong export-oriented specialist manufacturing and high corporate profits, is the powerhouse of the EU. Political dominance within the EU is assured not just by its economic prowess, but by the decline of French, Spanish and Italian economic power, as well as the isolationist path pursued by British Conservatives that ultimately led to Brexit.

The German perception that it foots the bills and assumes the burdens of leadership is true, to a certain extent. Yet to take this a step further, and claim that Germany is a benevolent force within the EU, is to enter the distorted world of the ordoliberals. There is no unitary European capitalism, and the political economies and monetary systems of the various EU member-states differ enormously – a fact that those who make the rules in the Eurozone wilfully ignore.[14] Germany's attempt to impose its model on the whole of Europe has been a major cause of the fractures that threaten the EU. The EU's macroeconomic policy works primarily in Germany's interests, as does the common currency: the EU provides the largest market for the export of German goods. In fact, the European Monetary System, as Perry Anderson points out, 'is a zone pivoting around the Deutschmark, the only currency never to be devalued within it ... For the first time in its history, the process of European integration is now potentially confronted with the emergence of a hegemonic power, with a widely asymmetrical capacity to affect all other member states'.[15]

Germany had cemented its hegemony (and its export capacity within the EU) by pursuing a deflationary wages policy in order to suppress internal consumption and manage the costs of reunification. This has had a knock-on effect in other EU economies, but the links between German economic dominance and a distressed and indebted periphery are obscured by the xenophobic media. During the Greek debt crisis, the tabloid newspaper *Bild* did more than most to promote a narrative that relied on xenophobia, running headlines like 'Stop! No More Billions for Greedy Greeks', 'The Greeks Are Begging for Our Billions' and 'Sell Off Your Islands, You Bankrupt Greeks, and the Acropolis Too'. Suddenly, the mainstream economic consensus that Germany's future lay in ever-closer European integration began to fall apart.

The Return of *Völkisch* Populism

All this initially served the interests of the AfD, a party that had gone through several transformations since it broke onto the political scene and could now, under the leadership of Alexander Gauland and Alice Weidel, be legitimately described as a far-right *völkisch* party. The original intention of its first batch of technocratic leaders was to build a right-of-centre broad church that would afford Germany – a country that had shaken off its fascist past – a greater role globally as a geopolitical power. Central to this vision was an 'orderly dissolution of the Eurozone' and the creation of smaller, more stable monetary unions. Citing the martyrdom of the Social Democrat banker Thilo Sarrazin (see Chapter 3) on the altar of political correctness, and using slogans such as 'Courage for the truth' and 'Courage to stand up for Germany', the AfD, backed (according to Robert Grimm's analysis of the AfD and the media) by *Bild* and the *Frankfurter Allgemeine Zeitung*, claimed that cosmopolitan elites ruling Germany were preventing a proper debate on the single currency.[16] But those who purported to speak for the 'German taxpayer', and argued that the restoration of the Deutschmark must not be 'taboo', soon saw themselves swept aside by the xenophobic current they had unleashed. By 2015, a younger, populist, less technocratic leadership – many of its members associated with the Christian right epitomised by its new leader, the Saxon entrepreneur Frauke Petry – had gained control of the party, buttressed by an influx of new members, many of whom were sympathetic to the Islamophobic and anti-immigration Pegida movement. At its 2016 annual meeting, the AfD stipulated in its new manifesto that Islam had no place in Germany. It has also called for Swiss-style plebiscites on asylum-seekers, mosques and minarets, attacked the burden that single mothers and the 'mentally handicapped' place on the economy, argued that asylum shelters should be shut down and the money put into teachers' salaries, as well as challenging adoption rights for homosexuals and suggesting that police should have the power to shoot refugees at the border. Now, with the election of Gauland and Weidel at the 2017 annual congress, the AfD, as in Poland and Hungary, is aggressively promoting memory wars. It advances its position in a country where the glorification of National Socialism is still a crime – and it does so in order to break taboos first, on the terms in which 'race' is discussed, and second, on the grounds of nationalism, suggesting a rewriting of the school curriculum to focus more on 'positive, identity-uplifting' episodes in German history, and less on Nazi crimes.[17] Frauke Petry may have resigned, citing the growing extremism of the party leadership, but it was she who first called for a re-evaluation of the term *völkisch*. This adds weight to Ulli Jentsch's characterisation of the AfD as a pre-fascist movement, the aim of which is to reform the political process and transform it into an authoritarian, *völkisch* system. Jentsch, one of the founders of NSU-Watch and the director of Apabiz, an anti-fascist documentation centre in Berlin, has studied the *völkisch* populist movements that first emerged in Germany in the 1890s, and whose ideas on militarism, blood and soil and the 'organic national community (*Volk*) – ideas developed in the context of the First World War – became openly anti-Semitic, and were linked to the rise of Nazism.

Southern Europe: The Legacy of Dictatorship

In southern Europe, grassroots movements organising around different aspects of the social crisis provided the groundswell for the electoral breakthrough of radical parties such as Syriza (2013) in Greece and Podemos (2015) in Spain. While the traditional centre ground of Spanish and Greek politics shows signs of distress, an examination of how the recent past impacts on the present suggests that national elites in both countries may adopt underhand, undemocratic methods to keep power.

After the Second World War, a nexus of police, military and oligarchs ushered in the southern European dictatorships that only came to an end in Greece, Spain and Portugal in the 1970s. The neo-Nazi Golden Dawn, which still has eighteen MPs in the Hellenic parliament (despite the mass arrests of its leadership on criminal charges), appears to have enjoyed the patronage of Greece's powerful shipbuilders. The party's penetration of the police and the military is one sign that, in Greece, the *diaplekomenoi* ('entangled ones') are pushing through again. Spain does not have the electoral equivalent of Golden Dawn, but the centre-right Popular Party is pushing through authoritarian laws. The 2015 Citizens' Security Law (popularly known as the gagging law or citizens' repression law) massively strengthened the powers of the police, who can now disband virtually any form of public protest, as well as fine those who afford them 'a lack of respect'. The Popular Party, which drafted the legislation, has been accused of taking Spain a step back towards dictatorship. Much of its support lies in traditional ultra-Catholic national elites, nostalgic for Franco.

Once again, an analysis of economic weaknesses in the context of German hegemony is crucial to an understanding of the defensive nationalism of old elites in Spain and Greece. Wolfgang Streeck has described how the Mediterranean countries developed a model of capitalism in which growth was driven not by exports and international competitiveness (as in Germany and much of northern Europe), but mainly by domestic demand, with borrowing and public expenditure used to stimulate growth.[18] The rigorous monetary policy of Germany does not suit the economies of southern Europe, which require monetary flexibility. But, a country having joined the Eurozone and accepted the convergence criteria, one model had to yield to another. The poorly regulated Spanish financial sector, which recklessly financed the rapid expansion of the banking sector through international borrowing, has been in deep trouble since the collapse of the property market and the bankruptcies of major companies in 2008. But Spain, the fourth-largest Eurozone economy, and therefore too big to fail, was spared the gruelling treatment meted out to Greece, receiving a €41 billion bailout under generous terms via the European Stability Mechanism.

The terms of Greece's third bailout (which came without any debt relief), laid out in the Third Memorandum, were, in contrast, draconian. Stigmatised, punished and reduced to penury, the Greek people woke up to the nightmare of a sovereign parliament dispossessed of power within a debtors' prison. 'Greece is now a semi-protectorate: a bigger Kosovo', argues Stathis Kouvelakis of the Left Platform, pointing to the loss not just of fiscal control but also of legislative power (all bills have to be approved by the Quartet – the old Troika of IMF, the European Central Bank and the European Commission, with the addition of the European Stability Mechanism – before being submitted to parliament).[19] As the economy shrinks and the debt burden increases, the Greek people face a bleak future of mass unemployment, home repossessions, shrinking pensions and collapsing public services. The most draconian austerity programme ever imposed on a European country was accompanied by the largest privatisation programme since the absorption of the GDR into West Germany. The Third Memorandum stipulated that public assets capable of being privatised, to a value equal to a quarter of Greek GDP, were to be pledged to the creditors. A privatisation fund in charge of real estate for the next ninety-nine years has been set up under the stewardship of EU officials, and an estimated 71,500 pieces of prime public property have so far been sold to pay off Greek debts. The biggest privatisation projects are the sale of two-thirds of the shares in the Piraeus Port Authority to the Chinese state-run China Ocean Shipping Company, and the lease of the operating rights to fourteen airports to a consortium led by the German company Fraport and Greek oligarch Dimitris Copelouzos. The majority of shares in Fraport are held by the federal state of Hesse and the city of Frankfurt, ensuring that the most profit-able Greek airports will boost the budgets of local authorities in Germany.[20]

Syriza has hung on to power, governing in an unlikely coali-tion with Independent Greeks, a right-wing anti-austerity party. The danger is that, without control of the economy and if sup-port from social movements and trades unions dwindles, Syriza will fall prey to the demands of pragmatism within a wider culture of curdled nationalism. Its previous principled humani-tarian stance towards refugees has already been undermined by the key role it must play in implementing the EU–Turkey migra-tion deal. And while the Syriza government may have had little choice but to accommodate to this, its managerial competence (including failure to pay the wages of the Greek asylum ser-vice workforce) has come into question. Another concern is that Panos Kammenos, the leader of Independent Greeks, is defence minister, and as such coordinates refugee support. While a change to the law allows the military to run closed detention and deportation camps at border entry points (most often in derelict warehouses on the Greek islands), the police continue to use excessive violence against refugees.[21] The expansion of the military into the civilian field, alongside the violence of immi-gration policing, is a cause for concern, not least because Golden Dawn had previously infiltrated the poorly trained border guard (as well as the riot police and sections of the military). Indeed, former Syriza finance minister Yanis Varoufakis warns that a 'combination of authoritarianism, permanent recession, defla-tion and racism' may embolden the 'dark forces' within.[22]

Spain: Migration, Precarity and Immigration Policing

Los indignados ('the Indignant Ones', also referred to as the 15-M Movement after the date of the demonstration that launched it) burst onto the political scene in 2011, focusing not just on austerity, but also on the need to end widespread political corruption. Organising against foreclosures and evictions, it was just one of many vibrant movements challenging Spain's national elites that have prospered under neoliberalism. From 2014 up to the rerun of the general election in June 2016, Podemos looked as if it could only grow as an electoral force. It was gathering in disgruntled voters from the Spanish Socialist Workers Party (PSOE), while the vote share of the right-wing Popular Party (PP) also declined dramatically in the 2014 general election. With the most fragmented parliament in Spain's history, another general election was called; meanwhile the country was left without an effective government. In the June 2016 election, the PP leader Mariano Rajoy projected himself as a defender of Spanish unity and continuity, opposed to a secessionist challenge in Catalonia. The strategy secured the PP the greatest share of votes, but still not enough to form a majority government. The fact that the general election took place just two days after the UK's decision to leave the EU may well explain the relative failure of United Podemos (its new name, reflecting its merger with other left-wing parties) to increase its share of the vote substantially. But the EU's humbling of an anti-austerity, left-wing Greek government also cast a long shadow.

However, to many it seems that Spain's electoral system, which promotes bipartisanship, is collapsing – with the threat coming not only from the radical left. Since 2011, the PP, which has traditionally absorbed voters from across the right-wing spectrum, has faced mounting challenges from the seventeen regional governments – particularly from right-wing separatist movements in Catalonia, which were pursuing nakedly anti-immigration, anti-Muslim agendas. In 2011, the conservative

Convergence and Union and the far-right Platform for Catalonia, founded by former supporters of General Franco, made
electoral gains on the back of extremist campaigns that blamed
immigrants and Gypsies for crime. In a region where you would
be hard pressed to find a woman wearing the full veil, the right
promised to ban the burqa and niqab as a preventive measure
'in case they come'. (PSOE politicians, too, supported the ban,
but in the name of gender equality.)

Spain is experiencing a declining birth rate, an ageing
population, and emigration of the highly educated (due to
austerity-driven cuts in universities and research institutions).
Over the last twenty years, it has relied on its migrant and
foreign-born workforce to drive up growth. Migration from
countries such as Ecuador, Bolivia, Romania and Morocco was
positively encouraged from 1999 onwards, the new workers
being heavily overrepresented in the construction, agriculture
and care sectors. But in the wake of the collapse of the housing market following 2008, the PP began to scapegoat migrant
workers, at the same time as substantially weakening their
position in the labour market through reforms that empowered
employers to reduce salaries and working conditions.

Prior to 2008, Spain was considered well integrated into
global financial markets, particularly through the internation-
alisation of Spanish companies buying up privatised public-sector
assets in Latin America. But the 'Spanish Bull', so dependent on
property development, and financial products, has lost much of
its virility through the bursting of the Iberian property bubble.[23]
Hundreds of thousands of low-income Spaniards who took out
subprime mortgages had their homes repossessed as a result, as
did relatives and friends who had guaranteed the mortgages.
Families of migrants were among the worst hit.

Disillusionment with the Socialist government's handling of
the economic crisis was growing (it had been the first to implement austerity), and in the 2011 general election the PP was
the main beneficiary, sweeping to power with a strengthened
majority. The PP not only deepened austerity, but introduced

unpopular labour laws aimed at creating a more flexible (in other words, precarious) workforce, prompting a general strike. Facing growing unpopularity, the PP turned to blaming migrants for the crisis, attacking the principle of universal healthcare free at the point of need. An April 2012 law excluded undocumented workers (except, in theory at least, children and pregnant women) from access to all but emergency healthcare. The government of Mariano Rajoy claimed that cancelling the health cards of 873,000 undocumented immigrants would save the country €500 million. This move was immediately challenged. Six of the autonomous regions refused to implement the law, and Doctors of the World launched a campaign, 'Right to Care', mobilising healthcare professionals, doctors and ordinary citizens. When it became clear that emergency services (far more expensive than a visit to a GP) could not cope with the extra demand, the prime minister announced a U-turn in April 2015, reinstating the right to primary care. But in August 2016 the Constitutional Court upheld the 2012 law, ruling that it was justified by the 'grave economic difficulty unprecedented since the creation of the National Health System', and that undocumented migrants' rights to human dignity and health were adequately protected by access to emergency care.

Migrants' sense of belonging had been seriously eroded. The attack on their access to the welfare state was accompanied by an accelerated removals programme and an increase in immigration policing. This had the effect of terrifying migrant workers and forcing them into a more clandestine mode of existence. As in the UK, the Spanish government sought to use immigration policy as a way to revitalise the 'boundaries' separating the 'citizen-worker' from the 'abject migrant', 'defining inside and outside, included and excluded', thereby paving the way for the 'creation and enforcement of internal bordering within the nation'.[24] These were all processes vital to the neoliberal plan to shrink the welfare state. At the same time, they expanded the powers of the immigration police – the least accountable policing body.

A Challenge to the 'Particracy'

The Spanish model of governance is unique in Europe. During an incomplete transition from dictatorship, political stability was prioritised over democratic governance as part of the 'Pact of Forgetting'. In 1977, an amnesty law gave immunity from prosecution to officials of the dictatorship and those who had carried out crimes during the Civil War. The idea was that 'moving on' was in the interests of the country's peaceful transition to democracy. The Popular Party was formed in 1989 from the Alianza Popular, built around former Franco minister Manuel Fraga. Spain, with its weak system of checks and balances within a diminished parliamentary democracy, has often been described as a 'particracy' – meaning that the two largest parties, one centre-right and one centre-left, dominate the state apparatus, carving out appointments to official bodies and to the judiciary. As a result, cronyism and corruption are endemic in public life, particularly in the parcelling out of public tenders at the local and national levels. Inequality, furthermore, has now become so extreme (Spain has the fourth-highest rate of childhood inequality in the EU after Romania, Bulgaria and Greece) that it constitutes a threat to public order, and elites now feel that the 'particracy' is under threat.

Historian Helen Graham fears that Spain will resolve its continuity problem through a revival of authoritarianism. She draws attention to the right's resort to the politicisation of historical discussion and its launch of memory wars which, she says, have a vehemence unsurpassed in Europe.[25] Ultra-conservatives within the PP have an overweening sense of their quasi-hereditary right to rule, she warns; they are responding to a loss of power by abandoning any lingering shame about their roots in dictatorship, aggressively challenging media documentaries dealing with the Franco era. Revisionist conservative historians are also on the publishing offensive, hoping to extract a serviceable past from the Franco period. Just as in Poland, any progressive reclaiming of history is challenged.

For Graham, it is vital that democrats defend instruments such as the European Convention on Human Rights as a way of restraining the worst instincts of those who continue to admire General Franco. There is a danger that fears about an 'uncertain economic future ... will arm ... an intransigent and socially intolerant ultra-nationalist politics far beyond its ideological core – and one whose consequences, however sleek and sanitised the "public spin", would be highly unpredictable and potentially lethal'.[26]

Colonial Continuities, Securitisation and the Market State

In no countries of Europe is the situation on the ground changing quite as quickly as in France and the UK. The right – whether Theresa May's post-Brexit hard-right Conservative Party or Marine Le Pen's Front National – is pulling at the heartstrings, exploiting all that is reactionary, jingoistic and xenophobic in French and British culture. In these old colonial powers, where a decline in international authority is concealed by bombastic rhetoric around British and French exceptionalism, racism and xenophobia are tied into the state itself. To argue that the extreme right is the main carrier of racism is to miss the point. Nativism has been woven into government policy in both countries. At the same time, divisive and chauvinistic 'one-nation' and 'republican' politics have singled out Muslims as the enemy within, which holds values antithetical to the nation. When the post-Brexit British government threatens to rid the NHS of foreign doctors and to use EU nationals as bargaining chips in negotiations, and when the French Republican Party's presidential candidate, François Fillon, echoes the anti-Muslim positions of Marine Le Pen, one may well speak of the *lepenisation* and *ukipisation* of French and British politics, respectively. The populist, anti-elitist idiom of the Front National (FN) and the United Kingdom Independence Party (UKIP) has done unspeakable damage to the progressive cause in both countries, both parties having made inroads into the working-class vote, mainly through the use of fear. 'Security' and 'counter-extremism' have become central to the diffuse forms of governance now practised in France and the UK, as they seek to maintain control in the face of deep social and economic cleavages. The logic of colonialism, its hierarchies and systems of domination, persist – this time on the battlefield of counter-insurgency and biopower.

Brexit and the Battle for the Working-Class Vote
Since 2012, the FN, UKIP and the UK's Conservative Party have aggressively targeted voters from the old industrial working class who previously voted for centre-left or even communist parties (in the case of France). Unlike the FN, the roots of which are in Poujadism and anger over the loss of 'French Algeria', UKIP emerged in the 1990s from within mainstream conservatism, essentially due to schisms over Europe. Nigel Farage, UKIP's leader in the run-up to the EU referendum, as well as the party's main donor, the multimillionaire insurance businessman Arron Banks, are both former Conservatives. Until 2015, UKIP had enjoyed mixed electoral fortunes. But 4 million people voted for UKIP in the May 2015 general election, when its share of the vote increased from 3.1 per cent to 12.6 per cent – expanding its base more than that of any other party, according to Richard Seymour, 'beyond its typical conservative southern England strongholds to the Labour-voting northeast, northwest and South Wales'.[27] In the May 2016 local elections, UKIP again scored well, breaking into the former mining valleys of Wales. Only in Scotland and Northern Ireland did it fail to secure a presence. As Seymour points out in his definitive article, it was only the peculiarities of the British electoral system that, at that moment, arrested the growth in UKIP's parliamentary presence. Now, however, the wheel has come full circle, many UKIP voters returning to a Conservative Party whose robotic leader very much talks their talk. Almost as verbally challenged as Donald Trump, May's chatter consists of a

few meaningless slogans – 'Strong and stable government' and 'Brexit means Brexit' being particular favourites.

But in France, despite the infighting that erupted between the northern and southern wings of the party after Le Pen failed to secure the presidency, the FN remains a potent threat. Since Le Pen took over the leadership of the party in 2011, it has implanted itself nationwide, securing twelve FN-backed mayors and 1,546 and 459 councillors (at the two levels of local government) since the 2014 municipal elections. Traditionally holding an annual demonstration on May Day, the FN describes itself as France's leading working-class party, going out of its way to target public workers and pensioners, seen as 'sensitive to a message emphasising the role of the state'.[28] Needless to say, UKIP and the FN could not have made such inroads into socialist and communist heartlands if the left had not abandoned them. The Socialist Party in France (PS), no longer a mass-membership party, may not even survive the election of Macron; and only the election of Jeremy Corbyn to the leadership of the British Labour Party revived its fortunes in that respect. Working-class voters had been taken for granted by both parties, which preferred to relate to them not through grassroots activism and public service but through PR companies, focus groups and media spin.

It was only after the June 2016 referendum on Britain's EU membership that the extent of working-class discontent in what is now routinely referred to as 'left-behind Britain' could be openly acknowledged. Former prime minister David Cameron's miscalculation in calling the referendum (so sure was he that his 'Remain' position would prevail) was matched only by the miscalculations of the official Britain Stronger in Europe campaign. Led by Cameron and shored up by Labour Party grandees, its pitch to voters was made on the basis of financial fear: corporate flight, declining house prices, and further austerity budgets were all promised should the Leave vote prevail. But the threat of another economic recession had little purchase in the former industrial heartlands, which were still deeply mired in the last one. What did resonate here (and it did equally, it should be said, in middle-class constituencies) was the anti-immigration vitriol of the right-wing press, owned and controlled by Eurosceptics. Adding a touch of glamour to the official Vote Leave cause were three high-profile Conservative politicians, Boris Johnson (a former London mayor and populist Euro-bashing journalist), Iain Duncan Smith (founder of the Centre for Social Justice, a New Right think tank) and Michael Gove (another former journalist and friend of Rupert Murdoch). Through a series of exaggerations, half-truths and downright lies, the official Vote Leave campaign lent political respectability to the anti-EU, anti-migrant cause – claiming, for instance, that hordes of Turkish migrants would enter Britain if it stayed in the EU, and that foreign rapists and criminals could not be deported because of EU legislation. It was left to UKIP, heading the unofficial Leave.EU campaign, to push the argument into explicit far-right territory. 'Islamist extremism is a real threat to our life', read a billboard after the Pulse gay nightclub massacre in June 2016 in the United States; another showed a long, snaking queue of migrants, adorned with the slogans 'Breaking Point: the EU has failed us' and 'We must take back control of our borders'.

A debate that could have been about how best to ensure economic justice and political accountability descended into a circus of xenophobia and nationalism. The fallout was immediately felt on the ground in the form of a huge increase in xenophobic and racist incidents, not to mention the murder, at the height of the campaign (in fact, one day after the 'Breaking Point' billboard) of Jo Cox, a Labour MP in West Yorkshire, by a white supremacist with connections to Britain First and the National Alliance in the United States. Cox was killed in a region where seven far-right parties have been actively terrorising Muslim communities for at least a decade – though, of course, analysis of the impact of the far right on the lives of ordinary Muslims was largely left out of the reckoning during the period of public grief over Cox's murder. In the same way, as the Institute of Race Relations shows in its report *Racial Violence and the Brexit State*,[29] the spike in 'hate crimes' that occurred in the immediate aftermath of the referendum was divorced by politicians and the media from its broader political content – namely, the divisive government policies on race, religion and migration, which had become its pump primer.

Cameron had not bargained for the vitriol of the *Sun*, the *Daily Mail* and the *Daily Express* (owned by UKIP financier Richard Desmond), as well as the more upmarket *Telegraph*, which all turned against him. Nor did he predict the betrayal by his erstwhile friends Duncan Smith, Gove and Johnson. This gang of three could draw intellectual ballast from a grouping calling itself Historians for Britain, which included David Starkey, Andrew Roberts and David Abulafia, and provided the ideological underpinnings for the notion that Britain could be great again if only it would 'take back control'. It was launched in the run-up to Brexit to promote the argument that the terms of EU membership were undermining British values. The historians laid out their case in a special issue of *History Today*, arguing that Britain had enjoyed a unique historical development as an 'island apart' from Europe, also asserting that 'the British political temper has been milder' and that anti-Semitism had never put down roots in Britain.[30]

Not surprisingly, across the water, FN leader Marine Le Pen was jubilant as the Brexit result was announced, tweeting 'Victory for Freedom' and promising to deliver Frexit should she win the next presidential election. As in the UK, the recent electoral successes of Marine Le Pen (now even more confident following Trump's victory and her securing of the official backing of *Breitbart News*) cannot be divorced from a general *lepenisation des esprits*. The hard-right populism of Sarkozy's Union for a Popular Movement (UPM, rebranded as Les Républicains in May 2015) and the complete capitulation of the Socialist Party (PS) on workers' rights have allowed the FN to capture former centre-left and communist territorial strongholds, presenting itself as the party of the working class. The FN had been languishing in the polls in the mid 2000s, but the War on Terror amplified its anti-Muslim message, while the reactionary policies of the Sarkozy and Hollande governments alike normalised Le Pen's authoritarian attitudes to law and order and racist urban policies. Without doubt, the disintegration of social democracy in France has been manna from heaven to the FN.[31]

The War Economy and the Decline of Influence
Even so, racism, nationalist populism and authoritarian attitudes in both France and the UK cannot be divorced from questions of the economy, or of the changing nature of the state itself. Media pundits in the UK see the Brexit result variously as a response to freedom of movement within a single market and to the failure of the left to speak to the concerns of the white working class (the black working class does not exist, it seems!). The UK is the sixth-largest and France the fifth-largest economy in the world, reflecting a switch in their positions since before the Brexit vote. But for how long? Manufacturing bases have been pulverised, industrial heartlands are in terminal decline, and business investment has dropped sharply as trades deficits mount. Both of these former colonial powers have an unrealistic sense of their continued importance in the world. Any possibility of coming to terms with the loss of global superpower status is undermined by the chauvinism and hubris that followed participation in wars in the Middle East, Libya, Syria, Afghanistan and, in the case of the UK, Iraq. Each country's defence sector benefits in different ways from war and conflict in the Middle East and North African region (MENA). The UK is the world's second-largest arms dealer and the world's fifth leading exporter of arms (Saudi Arabia is the premier market), supplying two-thirds of the weapons fuelling deadly conflicts in the Middle East. Only the United States is a bigger exporter. Firms such as the Anglo-Danish conglomerate G4S (the largest private security company in the world) boomed in

the aftermath of the invasion of Iraq, cashing in on outsourced operations, and the weapons industry as a whole is used as a lever to encourage foreign direct investment from the Gulf States. France too, with its colossal trade deficit, is dependent on arms exports to fuel trade, aggressively pursuing weapons sales in the Gulf and Asia. French multinationals, including defence companies like MBDA and Thales, also aggressively pursue French commercial interests within MENA. According to the economist Claude Serfati, France's major industrial groups, armed forces and political authorities form an 'armaments meso-system', with military muscle used to 'compensate for its declining economic influence'.[32]

When defence interests and foreign policy goals are interlinked, it is perhaps no surprise that racism and chauvinism are more openly expressed in public life. In both countries, powerful defence and private security industries now have inordinate influence on government policy. European participation in foreign wars, coupled with structural discrimination and an erosion of Muslim communities' sense of belonging, adds to a vicious cycle of reaction. A number of alienated young Muslims, having been exposed to the warped millenarian ideology of Islamic State (IS), are at war with society, seeking catharsis in acts of apocalyptic violence. IS recruits online, in chat rooms and through messaging services, benefiting also from the EU's failure to deal with its criminal underworld and clamp down on the black market in arms that accompanied the collapse of the Soviet Union.

Not surprisingly, reaction has been ratcheted up, primarily through the imposition of emergency measures once deployed in the colonies (house arrest, detention without trial, special courts, exclusion orders, deportation, suspension of civil liberties, and so on). Meanwhile, an all-pervasive narrative of national security serves to isolate critical voices, while a state-compliant Third Sector willing to spout government mantras about the dangers of extremism also helps to preserve the status quo.

The threat posed by IS – tragically played out first on the streets of London, then Paris, then Brussels, Nice, and so on – provides the excuse to lock down society still further. To date, most analysis of counter-extremism has focused, understandably, on its impact on Muslim communities. But counter-extremism has far deeper roots in Europe, going back first to colonialism, where it was used to justify the use of emergency measures against the 'unenlightened', and then to the Cold War. Counter-extremism has thus been a way of dividing the savages from the civilised, the enlightened from the benighted – a way of preventing groups from seeing and connecting with each other, thereby preserving the centre ground from true democratisation.

Securitising Education for the Neoliberal Era

The fear of extremist violence acts today as a powerful persuader, convincing the public that security for the majority can only be fixed by machine politicians of traditional political parties locking out the minority. It is in France and the UK, the countries where the lobbying power of the military and private security companies is at its strongest, that the counter-extremism security industry can be mobilised to isolate and marginalise autonomous social movements calling for more democratic participation. The UK's counter-extremism policies, based to a large extent on the co-optation of teachers, doctors and social workers into surveillance functions, are seen as a model to be followed by other European countries, plus Canada. In policy terms, most notably in criminal justice and education, the Conservative government is attempting to emulate the United States, where a deeply embedded culture of militarism has grown up in which the entertainment industries and schools provide the social structures and cultural conditions for military recruitment.[33] In short, counter-extremism is used today as a way of advancing the neoliberal agenda by securitising education.

Ever since the 2008 *Report of Inquiry into National Recognition of our Armed Forces*, there has been a blurring of the boundary between civilian and military spheres in the UK, the military having become more visible on the streets, in local communities and within the entertainment industries. But education, long penetrated by the short-term market values of neoliberalism, vocational goals and standardised test scores, is also a key area in which the government has attempted to impose a more hierarchical authority. Britain is the only country in Europe to recruit sixteen-year-olds into its armed forces, and the Department for Education continues to ignore UN recommendations that some form of peace education should be part of the curriculum in state schools.[34] In fact, the DfE is attempting to establish new illiberal norms within education through a number of measures, including the Military Skills and Ethos Programme (2011). This programme, first mooted by the New Labour think tank the Centre for Policy Studies, encompasses expanded cadet provision within state schools and the Troops to Teachers (TtT) programme (based on a US programme of the same name). TtT allows for the fast-tracking of former members of the armed service into teaching, in order to instil a military ethos into schools.[35] Other education-related government programmes include the Cadet Expansion Programme, launched in 2012, to expand military cadet units in schools; the Due Diligence and Counter Extremism Division within the DfE (2010); the 2014 requirement for all schools to promote Fundamental British Values (FBV) actively in the curriculum; and the July 2015 duty to prevent non-violent extremism in schools (under counter-terrorism legislation). All these developments, as well as the New Right's promotion of British exceptionalism (the 'island story') in debates on the teaching of history, will undermine liberal norms in education.

In a 2011 speech trailing the Troops to Teachers programme, Michael Gove, one of the architects of Brexit but then education secretary, argued that ex-soldiers recruited to teach or mentor school students would provide 'male authority figures' for an 'educational underclass' which, having grown up in a 'culture of dutiless rights', knew no 'civilised boundaries'.

These 'disruptive' young people display symptoms of cultural deprivation, Gove continued, including 'poverty of ambition', 'poverty of discipline' and a 'poverty of soul'.[36] With Gove self-destructing in the aftermath of his delusional bid to lead the Conservatives through Brexit, it has been left to the Ministry of Defence to fulfil his mission. In October 2016 the MoD announced the creation of twenty-five new cadet units for state schools. One school singled out for the Gove treatment was the Rockwood Academy in Saltley, east Birmingham. Under its former name of Park View Academy, the school was at the centre of the so-called 'Trojan Horse' scandal in 2014, when an anonymous letter named its Muslim chair of governors as part of an alleged plot by hardline Islamists to control the ethos of Birmingham schools. In September 2016, the school established both an anti-extremism programme and a Combined Cadet Force Unit programme under a full-time army officer, with the aim of instilling British pride in its pupils.

To date, the military ethos aspect of the Conservatives' education policy has gone largely unchallenged. But there are signs that its 'preventing non-violent extremism' agenda has placed such an inordinate strain on teacher–pupil and school–community relations that it may unravel. The Labour Party under Corbyn has committed itself to reform Prevent, making it more community-orientated.

Emergency Laws, Biometrics, and 'National Self-Defence'

But if, in the light of neoliberalism's clearly divisive impact, the attempt to mould a more passive, accepting population – less citizen, more subject – should fail, there is always the option of imposing a state of emergency. This change in governance is described by philosopher Giorgio Agamben as a state of exception, which is becoming a normal system of governance.[37] Agamben does not see this as a simple return to an authoritarian past. He argues, instead, that we are living through an epochal change. Governments no longer attempt to prevent problems, but merely to steer through them – not addressing, for instance, the causes of terrorism or migration, but their effects, since 'causes demand to be known', while 'effects can only be checked and controlled'.[38] This new mode of governance obliges states to treat each citizen as a potential terrorist or illegal immigrant, extending and multiplying controls and governing through digital and biometrical technology (ID cards, optical scanners, electronic passports, smart border-control systems, full body scanners, Automated Facial Identification Software, CCTV cameras – the list is endless). In this way, citizens (a political identity) become data (a biological identity), leading to a situation in which power has at its disposal unlimited biometric and other information on all of its citizens.[39]

A formal state of exception does not have to be openly declared, but a creeping and all-embracing securitisation – government by and through technology – takes place behind the scenes, making use of vague non-juridical notions like 'security reasons' to ensure a fictitious notion of an ongoing chronological crisis (as opposed to a single event demanding an emergency response). And it is out of ongoing national crises that those wielding state power can develop a powerful narrative that presents the state as the victim of the destabilising actions of the people, enabling them to frame its authoritarian reaction as merely a rational form of self-defence.

Nowhere is this clearer than in France. Following the massacre in Paris of 130 people by Islamic State sympathisers, the French prime minister Manuel Valls rounded on all those who 'seek excuses or cultural or sociological explanations for what has happened'.[40] *Laxisme* is the accusation now levelled by the state against those French men and women who believe that, in order to overcome terrorism, you must study its causes. French nationalism builds on the rhetoric of national self-defence – a mainstream discourse around loyalty, treachery and the belief that ends justify means. It plays on powerful emotions surrounding France's loss of prestige in the world – something that François Fillon attempted to capitalise on in his presidential campaign, promising to rewrite the history curriculum in order to tell the 'national story' of France and abolish an analytical focus on questioning French history, which he said was about 'doubting' France. The equivalent manoeuvre in the UK is the phrase 'taking back control', which has now been elevated into a political ideology. It similarly plays on feelings that Britain can be great again by ridding itself of foreign influence and staying true to its 'island story'.

At first glance, the French government's use of the state of emergency – its mobilisation of 7,000 troops for police operations under Operation Sentinelle – feels more like a redeployment of colonial rule within the metropolis. But, as if to prove Agamben's point about normalisation, in February 2016, not only did parliament vote to extend the state of emergency for a further three months, but the lower house also approved a proposal to enshrine powers to declare a state of emergency in the constitution. Popular opinion is behind the state of emergency, just as it was at the time of colonial rule, precisely because it is applied selectively and overwhelmingly (though not exclusively) against the *indigènes*: communities of sub-Saharan African and North African descent. A combination of Enlightenment fundamentalism (a totalitarian mindset against any expression of the Islamic faith) and the historical legacy of cultural assimilation and racial discrimination have proved fatal to democracy in a country that never came to terms with its colonial past, and now treats ethnic minorities not as equal citizens but as colonial subjects. They experience a colonial-style low-intensity-conflict policing in which a kind of military force is applied selectively and with restraint not to fight crime so much as to enforce compliance with the policies and objectives of the state. The colonial relationship between majority and minority is what Le Pen constantly seeks to exploit; she tapped into it during her presidential election campaign with repeated references to France's 'glorious history'. But she is not alone. The colonial mindset around minorities cuts across the political parties; the PS effectively took Le Pen's side when she attacked Emmanuel Macron for his half-hearted attempts to address France's colonial period and the war in Algeria.

In this way, a Socialist government created an authoritarian climate that gives the green light to the Brigades Anti-Criminalité, the Brigade de Recherche et d'Intervention (sometimes referred to as the 'anti-gangs brigade') and the Gendarmerie Nationale (a national police force which is a military corps with special powers to use guns without the restrictions imposed on other police officers) to act with impunity, terrorising and humiliating Muslims through raids on homes, meeting places and religious centres, all without judicial oversight. Power in France is increasingly arbitrary and authoritarian, as evidenced by bans on demonstrations, the use of assigned residency, calls for greater protection for police who shoot to kill (as in the UK), and – the final nail in the coffin – the detested El Khomri labour law, which is so unpopular that parliamentarians were denied a vote during its passage through parliament, and it was introduced by government decree. Research published by Amnesty International in May 2017 reveals the symbiosis between the anti-terrorism and labour laws; powers designed to combat terrorism have repeatedly been used to curb protest, as epitomised by the fact that, of 639 measures preventing named individuals participating in public assemblies, 574 were targeted at those protesting against proposed labour law reforms.[41]

Emergency laws include colonial-style house arrest, under which those suspected (but not formally accused) of radicalisation face a twelve-hour curfew, a ban on travel outside their municipality, and an obligation to report to the police up to three times a day – similar controls to those introduced in the UK in 2005, and modified in 2011.[42] All of this constitutes a form of collective punishment, on the basis of what a former president of the Lawyers' Union of France, Jean-Jacques Gandini, describes as 'prediction-based suspicion' – such orders being based on behaviour or associations, not on known criminal activities.[43] Gandini alerts us to the hybrid nature of the French state of emergency – looking back to colonial rule and forward to biometric rule (literally 'life measurement'), as the state of emergency allows the government to control and collect biometric and behavioural data on individuals whose identity traits have already assigned them to the category of being a security risk.

The idea that pride, patriotism and the nation-state itself are victimised by anti-colonial, non-majoritarian contestations of 'glorious history' is a central component of nationalism. Ideas of national victimhood are then used to usher in the 'strong state' – a state in which troublesome minorities know their place. One means of forcing assimilation into a dominant culture is to deny that structural inequality and institutional racism exist. But another way of achieving the same goal is to introduce into the discussion new hierarchies of race and class in which the white working class is placed at the bottom of the integration ladder, emerging as a forgotten 'ethnic tribe', and as the true victim of multiculturalism.

6

White Grievance and
the Cult of Exit

In *The Strange Death of Europe: Immigration, Identity, Islam*, the neoconservative associate director of the Henry Jackson Society and *Spectator* columnist, Douglas Murray, argues that not only did Tommy Robinson, the white working-class leader of the English Defence League, 'have a point', but that he was never treated fairly by the authorities, who chose instead a route of persecution and criminalisation. The cultural grievances of white working-class men are something of an obsession among media gatekeepers and cultural commentators like Murray. It is an obsession that provokes obvious questions. Why are issues of class being linked to skin colour? What is achieved by racialising the working class? Are there no black working-class, no Muslim working-class, or, God forbid, no multicultural working-class communities, experiencing the same problems of industrial flight and neoliberal abandonment? Are their grievances not of equal merit?

In the UK, many of those most attached to the 'white grievance' framework for explaining working-class support for the far right are part of a now powerful anti-extremism industry linked to government-orientated NGOs; they build on the views of the academic Roger Eatwell, who first penned the term 'cumulative extremism' to describe a spiral of 'reciprocal radicalisation', where one group brings out the worst in another in an enduring cycle of violence and terrorism. But others who have taken up the same refrain, like Blue Labour's Maurice Glasman, David Goodhart and Trevor Phillips, a former head of the Commission for Racial Equality, are influential cultural commentators with privileged access to the media. Echoing the New Right's attack on diversity, but influential this time in centre-left debates and liberal circles, they see white grievance (or essentially what can be seen as 'white extremism') as some sort of understandable backlash to multicultural state policies, failed integration and unlimited immigration. From their viewpoint, the working class has not been left behind because of deindustrialisation, capital flight and neoliberalism, but (in an argument that echoes another New Right attack – on cosmopolitanism) because the liberal elite favoured free movement of immigrants over protecting white workers' needs. And it is precisely this tendency – to treat white extremists as the passive damaged goods of global change and not actors in their own right or part of a multicultural working class – that has been embraced by the European Commission through its proselytising in favour of the Exit programmes for white supremacists that now exist in most European countries to provide inducements and support for fascists leaving the far-right scene. Such schemes operate without meaningful accountability or oversight, and reduce the struggle against fascism to a social programme, and one that has been depoliticised. Such programmes are often administered by the kind of private interest groups and government-orientated NGOs (GONGOs) that have flourished under the corporate modes of governance associated with neoliberalism, capturing political territory traditionally inhabited by civil society.[1]

A Component within Counter-Extremism Policy

Fascism is a political ideology that, in today's context, builds on a sense of majority victimhood and white grievance against so-called privileged racial minorities. It advances now through a political machinery that binds its supporters through acts of violence and the promise of the endless thrill of 'race war'. The fact that fascism is, by its very nature, violent is something that many people of colour and other targeted minorities in Europe understand only too well. It is they who have to clear up after a provocative march through their neighbourhood, live with the consequences of a brutal assault on a Saturday night, or have to flee when their homes or religious or community centres are set on fire.

Within the probation and prison systems there are strict guidelines for dealing with the perpetrators of any violent act (including racist acts); offenders have to address their offending behaviour and are not allowed to profit from past crimes. Yet, unbelievably, the European Commission (EC), via the counter-radicalisation strand of its counter-terrorism programme, has embraced a methodology (so-called Exit strategies) for dealing with white supremacism that goes against the grain of all other social policy on dealing with violent and criminal behaviour, even going so far as to treat fascist offending as a victimless crime.

In contrast to counter-radicalisation programmes for Islamists – whose grievances against Western foreign policy are not deemed legitimate but a symptom of their offending behaviour, proof that they are unwilling to de-link from Islamist ideology – the EC has fostered programmes that allow white supremacists to 'exit' the fascist scene while holding on to a key element of their former political ideology: their sense of white victimhood and grievance. The 'former' perpetrator of far-right violence is thus transformed into the victim of a harmful addiction or internal disease induced, in all probability, by a crisis in masculinity within the white working class. So the path is opened for the 'medicalisation' by European elites of the longstanding political problem of fascism within European societies, with interventions tailored to the psychological needs of individual clients. Such programmes to reset the cognitive behaviour and rewire the thought processes of maladjusted individuals are to be delivered by a Europe-wide industry of professional counter-radicalisation experts. Not only are these experts, some of whom are former neo-Nazis, vetted and promoted by the EC – they explicitly distance themselves from the values of anti-racism and anti-fascism, blaming anti-fascist movements for the unhelpful branding of neo-Nazis as racists and creating a hostile environment that hinders the successful exit from white supremacism.

In examining the whole counter-radicalisation industry that is developing around Exit and its clones, the recurring image is that of a house of cards. Exit's architecture is built on the shakiest of intellectual and ethical foundations. It is an industry that grows larger and larger, not united by philosophy or wisdom, or even tangible results, but balanced precariously on the flimsiest of foundations, and kept in place only by the vested interests of its key players.

The Roots of Exit

At the beginning of May 2014, the Swedish Ministry of Justice and the Institute for Strategic Dialogue co-sponsored a meeting in London on countering right-wing extremism. A primary aim was to explore the possibility of bringing Exit to the UK, to encourage white supremacists to disengage from the neo-Nazi scene. Such schemes were pioneered in Scandinavia in the 1990s, and then exported to Germany in 1998. The public disengagement of Stephen Yaxley-Lennon (who uses the pseudonym Tommy Robinson) and Kevin Carroll from the English Defence League (EDL) in October 2013 had given added impetus to those anxious to see the development of Exit programmes in the UK.

Exit is one of a number of counter-radicalisation schemes currently promoted in Europe. Another is the private-sector-led international network Against Violent Extremism (AVE), currently administered by the Institute for Strategic Dialogue in London, which had previously secured funding from the US State Department to carry out a feasibility assessment on the development of such a network. AVE was officially launched in 2012 at the Summit Against Violent Extremism in New York, and is the brainchild of Google Ideas founder Jared Cohen, a former adviser to both Condoleezza Rice and Hillary Clinton. It comprises a global network of 'survivors, activists, business people, experts and formers'.

It is the policy approach taken by EU home affairs commissioner Cecilia Malmström that has provided a boost for the development of such counter-radicalisation projects. In 2011, Malmström launched the Radicalisation Awareness Network (RAN) as part of the PREVENT strand of the EU counter-terrorism strategy. In January 2014, the European Commission identified ten areas in which member-states and the EU could improve their response to radicalisation and extremism, which included the proposal that all EU member-states set up de-radicalisation or Exit programmes for extremists, citing the positive impact such projects were already said to have had.[2] The European Network of Deradicalisation (ENoD), an alliance of twenty-six organisations from fourteen member-states, was officially inaugurated in November 2013, and includes representatives from Exit programmes in Germany, Italy (where Exit specialises more in workplace bullying and religious cults) and Sweden.

The roots of Exit in Sweden go back to the mid 1990s, when Sweden had earned itself an international reputation as one of the world's largest merchandisers of race-hate materials and the biggest exporter of 'white power' music to the rest of Europe. While fascists were arming themselves for 'race war', the anti-fascist magazine *Searchlight* warned of the dangers posed by ultra-liberal attitudes towards skinheads congregating at a

youth club within the Fryshuset centre in Stockholm.³ The neo-
Nazi scene was becoming more violent, yet naive social workers
at the centre were offering neo-Nazi skinheads 'fun' activities
such as military and supervisory guard training and coach trips
to white power music concerts across Sweden (racist concerts
were also held on the premises), as well as courses in desktop
publishing and newspaper production. The Fryshuset project
was financed by Stockholm City Council and backed by Social
Democrat politician Anders Carlberg, who believed that skinheads were definitely 'not racists', but 'fine lads' propagating a
'positive nationalism'.⁴

The skinhead youth club was the forerunner of the first Exit
programme, which was set up in the same Fryshuset centre in
Stockholm in 1998 and continues to this day, using many of
its original frameworks. But there was a pre-existing model in
the Norwegian 'Project Exit – Leaving Violent Youth Gangs',
hosted by the NGO and parental network Adults for Children,
established in 1996 by the Norwegian Ministry of Justice, the
Ministry of Children and Family, and the Directorate of Immi-
gration.⁵ In this case the ideological underpinnings of Exit
came from Dr Tore Bjørgo, a social anthropologist and lec-
turer at the Police Academy in Oslo. Bjørgo took research into
the formation of street gangs in the United States as a model
for understanding immigrant (ethnic) and neo-Nazi (white)
youth street activity in Norway.⁶ By divorcing the actions of
young neo-Nazi recruits from consideration of wider societal
norms and institutional structures, and virtually evacuating
white-supremacist movements of racist or ideological content
in his analysis, Bjørgo implied that anti-racism was as much
a problem as racism. He wrote that gangs tended to 'foster
rival gangs and successor gangs ... in an ongoing process', with
the impetus for Scandinavian gang formation in the 1990s
found within 'racism and anti-racism'. 'Militant anti-racism'
was blamed for its 'negative social sanctions' and 'branding'
of neo-Nazis, which in turn pushed youngsters further into the
stigmatised group, thereby 'diminishing their exit options and

strengthening their loyalty to the group'.[7] Similar thinking was evident at the May 2014 meeting in London mentioned above, promoted by the Swedish Justice Ministry, where there seemed to be a consensus among some participants that anti-racism was an obstacle to deradicalisation work with neo-Nazis. There was also the perception that state funding was available for youth work with black and Muslim kids, but not for the white working class. (The meeting was held under Chatham House rules, preventing the attribution of views to individual speakers.)

Controversies around Exit

From the outset, fascism across Scandinavian Exit programmes (including in Finland) was defined as a social, rather than a political, phenomenon. The neo-Nazi structures that young white Scandinavians joined were not the concern of Exit practitioners; their task was to wean youngsters from troubled backgrounds away from the identity problems arising out of destructive subcultures and family breakdown, which give rise, in Bjørgo's words, to a constant search for 'substitute families and father-figures'.[8] From this point of departure, programmes took on almost familial characteristics. Neo-Nazis were treated as lost sheep, or white 'prodigal sons', to be reintegrated into the Scandinavian national community through models of intervention that appealed to their sense of victimhood and grievance. That anti-racists branded their charges as racists and fascists made their task, they asserted, that much harder.

Although current national Exit programmes in Sweden, Norway and Germany are independent of each other, there is a common strand. Information about Exit's current activities is tightly controlled, and past failures and controversies are simply passed over. According to Tor Bach, editor of the Norwegian anti-fascist magazine *Vespen*, the original Project Exit, hosted by Adults for Children, was a total failure from start to finish. 'This project was run in South Norway, in Kristiansand', he says. 'Ridiculous claims focusing on exaggerated successes were constantly made, but all the time, the Nazi milieu was growing.'[9] Bach also observes how, over the years, Exit practitioners claimed success for preventative work that was in fact carried on outside Exit, principally by dedicated police and youth workers, many of whom preferred to stay quiet about any successes.

The first full-blown version of Swedish Exit, set up in Stockholm within the Fryshuset in 1998 under the directorship of former neo-Nazi Kent Lindahl, initially sparked a great deal of controversy.[10] In 2001 there was a bitter dispute with a sister organisation in Motala, run by social worker Anita Bjargvide, who accused Stockholm Exit of lacking proper oversight. She suggested, among other things, fraud in accounting: the organisation, she claimed, was deliberately inflating the numbers of defectors it purportedly helped in order to secure more government funds. She also said that inappropriate language was being used on the premises, including racist jokes, and that, on occasion, white power music was played.[11]

Today, similar criticisms are still being made within antifascist movements about the values and methodology of Exit programmes across Europe. There is still confusion about Exit's functions, as well as a lack of clarity about the way its organisations are formally constituted and managed. Describing themselves variously as foundations or NGOs, but firmly tied into state funding and counter-radicalisation programmes, some of the staff are former neo-Nazis (the official term in Germany is *Aussteiger*, which roughly translates as 'dropouts'). Transparency seems to be lacking, and there are none of the checks and balances that would exist if former neo-Nazis were rehabilitated for past crimes through the probation process, for instance.

'Drop-Out' Programmes in Germany

In the post-war Federal Republic of Germany, membership of fascist parties (as well as communist ones) was deemed unconstitutional, and although communist and fascist parties were not banned, those who joined were drawn to the attention of the Federal Office for the Protection of the Constitution (Bundesamt für Verfassungsschutz, BfV) and prohibited from working in the civil service under the *Berufsverbot* decree. It was against this rarefied, hyper-securitised historical background that Exit-Deutschland was co-founded in 2000 by the prominent east German former neo-Nazi Ingo Hasselbach and the criminologist and former police detective Bernd Wagner, with the support of two highly respected independent foundations.[12] In addition, in 2001, various other state-controlled Exit schemes were established under the *Aussteiger* programme. This federal programme also runs in prisons, where participating neo-Nazis enter the witness protection scheme and can obtain certain legal advantages.[13] The BfV also runs its own scheme for 'drop-outs', the methods of which are unclear, although the number of *Aussteiger* participating is published annually.

German practitioners working with the victims of far-right violence feel that participation in the various Exit schemes, whether governmental or non-governmental, is now too easy an option. Bianca Klose, head of the Mobile Counselling Team against Right-Wing Extremism Berlin (Mobile Beratung gegen Rechtsextremismus Berlin, MBR) feels that, while Exit schemes run by NGOs are necessary and can accomplish much, there is a danger that, by placing too strong an emphasis on the perpetrator (in terms of both funding streams and public education), the wider debate about society's responsibility for the growth of the far right can get lost, while the victim's perspective becomes muted. She also has misgivings about some high-profile stories about success cases.[14] Exit statistics purporting to show the success of deradicalisation programmes cannot really be tested. First, without meaningful oversight, who is to say that the statistics presented by the Exit practitioners (vital for securing more funding) are accurate? Second, statistics purporting to show success are almost meaningless if there is nothing to compare them with. Who can say, for instance, that better results would not have been achieved by placing equivalent amounts of money into youth work, catching youngsters at the periphery of such groups before they get sucked in?

Klose has some thirteen years of professional experience working with the victims of far-right violence. While recognising that the parents of young white supremacists might well need organisational support in order to challenge and 'win back' their children, her working life has also taught her how manipulative right-wing extremists can be in order to be taken up as an *Aussteiger* – particularly if this serves the purpose of reducing a sentence or securing probation. Too often, 'they pretend to leave the scheme, only to return, once they have secured the desired outcome', concludes Klose. This sort of deception could be curtailed through a higher standard of evaluation, as well as more thorough monitoring and supervision that included the requirement that clients make full acknowledgement of past crimes, provide information on neo-Nazi structures or the criminal – or even terror-related – activities of their members.

For Klose, the key issue is how Exit schemes are implemented. She is adamant that NGOs have a role to play in helping neo-Nazis turn their back on fascist ideology, but is concerned about the creation of an 'expert class' of former neo-Nazis, some of whom go on to develop professional careers as coaches for the *Aussteiger* or are employed as consultants or trainers in violence prevention. 'This is something that we see quite often', she says. 'Soon after leaving the scene, they are brought before the public and treated like experts, thus mixing the biographical with the professional … blurring the distinction between two areas of life which are really quite distinct.' Leaving the scene is not in itself proof that a person has dealt with his ideology or come to terms with his actions; this question needs to be examined in a far more sustained and sensitive manner. But 'way too quickly, they are invited into schools and workshops'. There is now the rise of a whole genre of confessional political-conversion literature, and some of the 'drop-outs' even go on to become celebrities.[15]

What Becomes of 'Formers'?

Many of Klose's observations echo concerns expressed in the UK at the time of the much-publicised exit of Tommy Robinson and his cousin Kevin Carroll from the EDL in 2013. Ever since Robinson co-founded the street-fighting EDL in Luton in 2009, the media, with its constant interviews and media profiles, has given him the oxygen of publicity, thereby downplaying the impact of the EDL's violent demonstrations through Muslim neighbourhoods across England. Predictably, the TV, radio and print media were there in force in October 2013 when the Quilliam Foundation organised a press conference for Tommy to bare his soul about the reasons he was deserting his former EDL comrades. As Matthew Goodwin perceptively observed at the time, his resignation 'was remarkable' as much for what did not happen as for what did – namely, 'a remarkable display of disingenuous nonsense, backed up by the counter-extremism think-tank the Quilliam Foundation … There was no repudiation of the EDL's beliefs, or goals. There was no criticism of EDL foot soldiers', who were held up by Robinson as 'decent … the best people in my life'.[16] Time has certainly proved Goodwin right. Since Robinson's highly publicised exit, and his subsequent imprisonment for mortgage fraud, he has enjoyed a brief spell in the British Freedom Party, rejoined the EDL, formed Pegida UK, been photographed carrying a gun while sitting on an Israeli tank on the Golan Heights, and fallen out badly with the Quilliam Foundation.

Robinson, in particular, is a media celebrity – one who has added in his autobiography, *Enemy of the State*, his own action-man take on the confessional memoir genre. But the story of a different 'former' may throw light on Robinson's alleged exit from the far-right scene. Nick Greger was a German neo-Nazi with a long history of terrorist activity. He was an associate of Carsten Szczepanski, a paid neo-Nazi informant who has given evidence in the NSU trial (see below), and who was initially recruited by the intelligence services while in prison serving an eight-year sentence for the attempted murder of a Nigerian man. Greger's trajectory is murky, to say the least. In 2005, he was helped by the federal version of German Exit to write a confessional account of his disengagement from the neo-Nazi scene. His 'conversion', however, was seemingly short-lived. Greger went on to become a leading light within the counter-jihad movement in the UK, founding, alongside Paul Ray, Order 777, which supported Anders Breivik.[17] But was this really a story of a racist dropping out from the neo-Nazi scene, only to drop back in as a fully fledged counter-jihadist espousing apparently equally far-right views? Or is something else going on? It is not inconceivable that Greger, who now lives comfortably in Gambia, was placed on the German secret services' payroll when he dropped out in 2005. Might he even have been working with the British secret services when he founded Order 777? On these questions we can only speculate.

Exit Programmes Versus Justice for the Victims

It is this murky terrain of state secrets, spy rings, and possibly faked conversions that those working to mitigate the impact of violent racist activity in Germany have to navigate on a day-to-day level. Their positions – against racism and fascism, and for justice for the victims – are not necessarily those most favoured by the state. In fact, Exit programmes side-line anti-racist approaches in favour of more muted ones based on the perspective of anti-extremism, promoted by government-sponsored former neo-Nazis who, unlike their victims, have never been at the receiving end of racist violence, and yet are now treated as experts on the roots of prejudice.

The role of the distorting practices of the secret services is crucial. Just who exactly are these *Aussteiger*? And could their accounts of conversion be either self-serving, partial (designed to hide a larger truth) or just plain lies? Take the trial of Beate Zschäpe (the sole surviving member of the NSU neo-Nazi terror cell) and her four co-defendants. Lawyers for the victims and groups like NSU-Watch who have monitored the trial dispute the official narrative that the NSU was an isolated cell consisting of three people aided by four unimportant accomplices, insisting that it was a complex of interests involving many more people, including Blood and Honour in Saxony, which provided safe houses, passports and medical assistance, and even tried to procure weapons for Zschäpe and her dead comrades Böhnhardt and Mundlos when they went on the run in 1998. As the scandal surrounding the intelligence services, the police and the NSU deepens, is it possible that some *Aussteiger* know more about the NSU than they are prepared to reveal publicly? In *Homeland Security: The State and the NSU Murders*, journalists Stefan Aust and Dirk Laabs convincingly demolish the argument that the intelligence services were 'blind in their right eye'.[18] Given the number of paid neo-Nazi informants they were running, it was impossible for them not to have known about the far right's potential for terrorism. In recent dramatic developments, the German national television network ARD has alleged that the leader of Blood and Honour, Stephen Thomas Lange, was recruited by the BfV in 2002. In exchange for informing on the organisation's structures after it was banned (alongside Combat 18) in 2000, Lange (codenamed 'Pinocchio') was allegedly offered protection and shown leniency for past crimes. According to Left Party politician Andre Hahn, if the revelations proved correct, it would mean that the BfV had not been monitoring the group, but 'steering it itself'.

By having paid neo-Nazis as informants, the BfV and the

police may now find themselves implicated in the crimes of the NSU complex – particularly if they are judged to have failed to pass on 'deadly intelligence' supplied by these informants to the Federal Office of Criminal Investigation. But what actually constitutes 'deadly intelligence'? It is in the context of British state collusion with loyalist paramilitaries in Northern Ireland that the clearest definitions of collusion and deadly intelligence have emerged. For Paul O'Connor of the Pat Finucane Centre in Derry, deadly intelligence is 'information which deliberately puts lives at risk; should have been used to save lives; or is used to smear the victim in the media, thus lining them up as a potential target for attack'.[19] Now working with lawyers for the NSU victims, the Belfast-based Committee on the Administration of Justice is pressing for the conduct and behaviour of the handlers of informants to be brought under the framework of international law. Deputy Director Daniel Holder argues that 'you can't have a situation whereby particular persons are protected because they are close to the state and its interests at the expense' of others, whose lives are 'seen as dispensable and not worthy of protection'.[20] One case that vividly demonstrates the lack of moral compass and callous indifference to the victims of far-right crimes is that of Tino Brandt, a former vice-chair of the NPD in Thuringia, and one of the founders of Thuringia Homeland Security, from which the NSU emerged. Until Brandt was exposed by the media as a paid informant in 2001, he had been one of the intelligence services' most prized assets, believed to have been paid more than $132,000 for information supplied between 1994 and 2001 – money he reinvested back into the neo-Nazi scene. In 2014, Brandt, who was called to give evidence at the NSU trial, was sentenced to over five years in prison on charges relating to over sixty-six cases of sexual abuse of minors, including rape and prostitution, carried out between 2011 and 2014. Did the intelligence services know that Brandt was a rapist and paedophile? The file on Brandt's activities for the security services, which may have revealed the answer to this question, was one of the many documents and files on the paid-informer scheme that were reported missing or shredded in January 2012, on the eve of the cross-party parliamentary commission of inquiry into the NSU case – an inquiry that had the power to scrutinise all documents and files of the security services.

In this context, lawyers for the NSU's victims are entitled to speculate further about BfV Exit programmes, particularly in prisons. We now know that at least one informant, Carsten Szczepanski, the associate of Nick Greger referred to above and a former KKK Grand Dragon in Brandenburg, was recruited by the secret services in Brandenburg just prior to receiving an eight-year prison sentence for a brutal gang attack on a Nigerian man who nearly died of his injuries. In 1994, while Szczepanski was still on remand awaiting sentencing, he offered to inform for the secret services and was subsequently released early (on grounds of good behaviour), after which he was involved in many racist and terrorist crimes, including weapons procurement and assembling bombs – all, seemingly, while he was on the security services' payroll.[21]

The German and Swedish intelligence services appear to take different approaches. NSU-Watch is currently building up a detailed picture of the Scandinavian connections to the NSU complex, particularly through Blood and Honour, which similarly acts as a network and may have supported the murderers while they were on the run. But there is no evidence that the Swedish intelligence services are remotely interested in the question of whether Scandinavian fascists assisted the NSU. The German intelligence services did want to penetrate and control the far-right scene, although their motivation for doing so would appear unrelated to crime prevention, and is frankly, in the absence of transparency (and despite several parliamentary inquiries), incomprehensible. But the Swedish intelligence services appear to have little interest in infiltrating the neo-Nazi scene, continuing the security services' 1990s approach of burying their heads in the sand about the danger that right-wing extremists pose.

In Sweden today, Exit practitioners build on the earlier 'lost sheep' approach to racist skinheads adopted by their first controversial patron, Anders Carlberg. He in turn had been influenced by the American Jungian prophet poet Robert Bly's thesis on 'positive maleness and nationalism'.[22] Exit Sweden, run by the former white supremacist Robert Orell, is today located within the same Fryshuset youth centre of old, and continues to focus on white victimhood.[23] While Orell describes himself as a former 'white supremacist' who was active in the violent skinhead scene in the 1990s, there is nothing to indicate what (if any) violent acts Orell (who describes himself as a trained psychotherapist) committed during that period of his life, or whether any suffering he may have caused to others through his actions has been acknowledged through acts of sympathy, commitment and action.[24] In fact, a thorough Internet search yields nothing specific about Orell's past activities at all. While there may be a simple explanation for this, the lack of public information available on Orell's past activities leaves a disturbing impression.

According to an evaluation of the work of Exit Fryshuset carried out by the Institute for Strategic Dialogue, the organisation is staffed largely by 'former white supremacists', and their work is 'based on long-term cognitive treatment that assists in the protracted disengagement process'.[25] Its methodology for working with 'formers' starts from the premise that individuals who join white-supremacist movements do not join for ideological reasons – in other words, that it is seldom a positive choice based on political convictions. By this they mean, presumably, that the 'formers' were never really Nazis, and definitely not racists! Instead, they are attracted to white-supremacist movements for emotional and psychological reasons, as they felt excluded or unaccepted by mainstream society and were searching for 'identity, support and power'. Today, white supremacists who contact Exit are told that they will benefit from a 'non-judgmental' approach that focuses on their 'grievances' and not their 'ideology'. Hence, Exit does not deal with ideology, or tackle political views head-on, but focuses on resentments, encouraging 'clients' to change their lifestyles and develop greater self-esteem.

Attempting to comprehend the Exit strategy is like investigating a cult, or an experiment in mind games. Certainly, the devotion of many to an Exit discipline that seems so devoid of genuine content is puzzling from the outside, as is the idea that society can be changed by a programme of conversion and re-wiring of individuals. One counter-radicalisation professional wedded to the Exit brand told me privately of her unease at witnessing former neo-Nazis at international counter-radicalisation conventions being treated with all the veneration of ageing rock stars. Clearly, there is some disquiet within the Exit house of cards.

There are various parties, with very different interests, who operate within the strictures of Exit. These include former neo-Nazis, professional youth workers, civil servants attached to the EC, analysts from counter-radicalisation think tanks, the global elite at Google Ideas, secret service handlers and neo-Nazi informants. Obviously they do not all share the same perspectives or interests.

Only diehard authoritarians (or fascists) would deny that human beings have the capacity to change, to learn through past experiences, and to grow. The desire to remould criminal justice systems so that past offenders, viewed as intrinsically bad, are branded ad infinitum for past violence, is a philosophy that has no place within progressive politics. So it is sad to see a situation where youth workers and liberals with lofty ideals about human transformation have been seduced by the psycho-babble of the Exit brand. Their failure to understand the political and societal roots of racism and fascism hardly serves their clients if it leaves them mired in the fascist pigsty of white victimhood and grievance. Besides which, as part of the normal course of things, and without public fanfare or media glory, youth workers, teachers, probation officers and anti-fascist organisations have made it their business to assist young people manipulated by the far-right to take responsibility for their actions and support them when they exit the scene. But what of the more powerful interests? European elites today are faced with a growing anti-racist movement, particularly among the young, that connects fascism with institutionalised racism and government policy. For governments, the promotion of an apolitical and easily malleable counter-radicalisation industry that distances itself from anti-racist, anti-fascist values is a very desirable option. 'Invisible government' is defined by John Pilger as the unseen mechanism of society whereby organised habits and opinions are manipulated, particularly by domestic intelligence and security agencies, which can be backed by corporate and media interests.[26] Today, questions about the hidden hand of 'invisible government' and the nature of covert policing (the policing you do not see) are also essential for those who want to examine the role of Exit within state counter-extremism policy more closely. The security sector, not surprisingly, plays a central role within the counter-extremism industry. Now, with at least half of the world's population living in countries – including the UK, Germany and Poland – where there are more private security workers than public police officers, the security sector's reach extends still further. As the EU moves to stem population movements that are the direct result of war and conflict, private security companies also play a greater role than ever before in the management of asylum and immigration systems, and in the violation of human rights.

IV.

Securitisation and Resistance

7

The Market in Asylum and the Outsourcing of Force

In 2015, over 1 million people arrived in Europe from countries such as Syria, Iraq, Afghanistan and Eritrea. They had crossed through the so-called Balkan and Arctic land routes, or by sea, many of them losing their lives in the southern Mediterranean as they set sail from Turkey and Libya in inflatable dinghies, or wooden or fibreglass boats. As EU member-states bickered over who should take responsibility, particularly over the boat people cast ashore in Greece, Italy and Spain, a European community of civilian volunteers appeared, seemingly from nowhere, to feed, clothe and shelter the refugees. But care, compassion and human solidarity could only go so far. As the numbers of the sick, exhausted and desperate swelled, and dangerous bottlenecks emerged for the refugees, politicians were called on to govern and EU bureaucrats to act. German Chancellor Angela Merkel took the first decisive step. By announcing the suspension of the Dublin regulation (for Syrians), she opened up a humanitarian corridor to funnel Syrians from Greece to Germany.

But Merkel's intervention was just a momentary ray of light over pools of darkness. Soon EU leaders returned to their petty squabbles, failing to live up to responsibilities laid out by the European Council of Ministers in the EU's modest plans to relocate 160,000 refugees from Greece and Italy across member-states. Hungary, which lay on the path of the Balkan migration route, declared a 'state of migration emergency', erecting a 109-mile razor-wire fence at its border with Serbia, initially costing €98 million – at least three times the €27.5 million budget of its Office of Immigration and Nationality, though costs were rapidly rising. Other countries in the region – Macedonia, Croatia and Serbia – were quick to follow suit. By mid 2016, the western Balkan route into Europe was closed, leaving thousands stranded in Greece.

Externalising the Crisis and Militarising the Border

Western and northern European heads of state tend to speak in less obviously racialised terms about refugees than the likes of the Hungarian prime minister Viktor Orbán, who routinely describes all refugees as Muslims and all Muslims as terrorists. Deploying a more flowery vocabulary, they maintain the fiction that Europe is the continent of liberalism, generosity and the rule of law. At the same time, and in ways that are no different from eastern Europeans, they are putting up the barricades: the Danes have introduced military-style controls on the Øresund railway and motorway bridge across the Øresund strait between Sweden and Denmark; the Norwegians have erected a new gate and fence, 200 metres long and 3.5 metres high, at the Storskog border point with Russia; and the British paid £2.3 million to build a four-metre-high wall running for 1 kilometre along both sides of the main road to Calais. The EU has sent warships to the Mediterranean to turn boats back, borders have been fortified to prevent any forward movement, and migrants – thanks to the European Commission's 'hotspots' (see below) – have been forced into open-air prisons on the Greek islands and in Italy. European police forces and militaries – east and west, south and north – have acted violently to police and forcibly evict desperate migrants living in makeshift camps, most notably at Idomeni in Greece and Calais in France. Meanwhile, vigilante and paramilitary squads have been allowed to do the dirty work that democratically controlled law enforcement agencies cannot be seen to do.

In March 2016, the EU brokered an unprincipled deal with Turkey. The aim was the closure of the eastern Mediterranean route to Greece, and the deal allowed first for the deportation of all migrants considered not in need of international protection, and, second, for the so-called 'one-in, one-out' solution for Syrian refugees (for each Syrian returned to Turkey, one would be selected for resettlement from Turkey's refugee camps). Amnesty International characterised this as the 'bartering of refugees' – a reference to the €3 billion and other financial and trade incentives that Turkey received in exchange for its human cargo. After the attempted coup in Turkey in July 2016, and the escalation in state oppression, there is a possibility that the EU–Turkey deal will fall apart. Some suggest that Greece will become a huge holding pen for asylum seekers, Europe's equivalent of what Nauru is to Australia.

The EU–Turkey deal represented the norm, the 'European way' of externalising the 'crisis' and militarising the border. But at the same time it provided yet another opportunity to outsource the punishment, processing and care of asylum seekers and migrants to private security companies. It is a response in keeping with the creation, over at least three decades, of an integrated, transnational system of surveillance and spatial control to slow down, filter, block, contain, warehouse, process and mark out those from the Global South worthy (or unworthy) of the benefits of European civilisation and 'hospitality'. Of course, all countries practise immigration controls. But in an era of globalisation, the rich industrialised nations have colluded in the creation of a global system of migration controls that serves the interests of market-states and global elites, at the same time as demonising the poor and the persecuted and excluding them from the culture of human rights. Some commentators characterise this as global apartheid: the limitation of people's freedom of movement based on nationality.

Market Values and Neoliberal Abandonment

Whether detained or dispersed under national asylum systems, migrants and asylum seekers, far from being a burden on Europe, are an occasion for profit, prising open markets for private equity groups and security companies. And here the moral panics orchestrated over foreigner crime serve a very useful purpose. They obscure an important fact: that the rich North has abandoned refugees and migrants to the free market – a strategy that goes hand in hand with state-sanctioned harm and violence, including cruel and degrading treatment and torture. The sociologist Avery Gordon, who sees strategies of abandonment as integral to neoliberalism, defines abandonment as a process whereby the state systematically and in an organised fashion devotes resources, financial or otherwise, to the development of an infrastructure for warehousing and disposing of populations deemed surplus (making them so in the process), rather than taking care of them through education, job training and placement, public health services or other forms of social investment.[1]

So, first, private security companies profited from the growth in systems to contain, detain and deport asylum seekers, foreign-national offenders and immigration 'overstayers'. Now, many of the same companies that profit from the punishment end of the market profit, too, from 'protection', as new markets in the care sectors, traditionally the responsibility of government, are opened up. In 2014–15, according to a Freedom of Information response, support to asylum seekers in the UK cost £234 million, including staffing and administration costs.

Thus, as Jonathan Darling has shown in relation to the way that UK private providers have spread from deportation to accommodation regimes, 'framing asylum seekers as a burden' obscures the production of an 'asylum market'. Created via 'processes of privatisation, contractualism and the outsourcing of state responsibilities', it gives rise to 'new assemblages of authority, policy and governance'.[2] As Ferguson and Gupta explain, this represents 'not so much a "rolling back" of the state, but a "transfer of operations of government … to non-state entities"', thereby producing not 'less government', but rather 'a new modality of government'.[3]

Across the North, the asylum and migration market is creating jobs, mostly in the field of border control and security, where power is shared between states, inter-state bodies, immigration police, the military, and private companies developing new surveillance technologies. The European Agency for the Management of Operational Cooperation at the External Borders of the Member States of the European Union, known as Frontex, which was set up in 2004 (now the European Border and Coast Guard Agency, EBCG), has quickly evolved from an inter-state project into a large and ever-expanding EU agency, with 402 staff in its Warsaw office (set to increase to 1,000 by 2020). It operates on a huge budget, which was increased in 2016 by 54 per cent to €176 million. In July 2015, an ambitious plan was approved by the European Parliament to expand its competences. Previously, Frontex was meant to bolster member-states' border forces' surveillance and detection capacities; in future it will work alongside the EU's Mediterranean naval force EU NAVFOR, which is now training Libyan coastguards within the framework of Operation Sophia. The initial proposal would have given the agency the power to override domestic border forces when they are perceived to have failed, but it was defeated. A primary function of its new permanent 'rapid reaction' corps of 1,500 border guards will be to organise and coordinate deportation operations. But Frontex has a surveillance function, too. National coordination centres pump intelligence into its Situation Centre in Warsaw, where algorithms identify patterns and trends in order to develop 'a system of systems' capable of delivering 'frictionless circulation of … data within a single globalised market of information'.[4]

Despite this, or perhaps because of it, record numbers of migrants are drowning in the Mediterranean. According to the Missing Migrants Project within the International Organization for Migration (IOM), there was a 67 per cent increase in deaths in the Mediterranean in the first six months of 2016. The UN High Commissioner for Refugees points out that, in the year that followed Alan Kurdi's death, an average of eleven people have died each day in the Mediterranean sea, of whom two are children. Certainly, many Greek, Italian and Spanish coastguards do make heroic efforts to save lives; but their political masters have other priorities – namely, the 'war against smugglers', through gunboats, if necessary. At first, politicians did not move against the humanitarian search-and-rescue operations carried out by groups such as Médecins sans Frontières (MSF), Save the Children, the Hellenic Rescue Team, Sea-Watch and the Migrant Offshore Aid Station. The Bourbon Argos, one of three merchant ships hired by MSF for rescue operations, rescued more than 20,000 people in an eight-month period ending in December 2015. But as the total securitisation of the Mediterranean sea route has become the only policy goal, EU member-states have once again started to use laws against trafficking and smuggling to criminalise those acting from humanitarian motives. In one case, three Spanish firemen, Manuel Blanco, Enrique Rodríguez and Julio Latorre, volunteer lifeguards for the NGO Professional Emergency Aid, launched a rescue mission for a sinking boat, only to find themselves prosecuted by the Greek government as human traffickers.

The Expansion of Immigration Policing

At the same time, in line with the growth in aliens' policies (see Chapter 2), immigration enforcement agencies have seen their budgets, influence and powers multiply. This expansion of the powers of the immigration police (both at borders and within countries) is in line with developments noted by international security expert Peter Andreas in 2003.[5] Free trade and economic liberalisation, he argued, fundamentally change the function of borders. Inevitably, accords like the Schengen Agreement (which abolished border controls between all EU countries, save Ireland and Britain) mean that borders cannot operate only as barriers, but must work as filters, guaranteeing legitimate border crossings (for business and the wealthy) while keeping out 'undesirables' (refugees). It was the need for the border to act simultaneously as security barrier and economic bridge – a state-of-the-art electronic border filter – that gave rise to technological innovation. Thus, the so-called 'smart border' blurred the line between external and internal security, requiring, in Andreas's words, more 'tracking and control mechanisms beyond the point of entry (i.e. a "thickening" of borders and the creation of buffer zones); and in some places, growing use of military and intelligence hardware, personnel, and expertise for policing tasks'.[6] Hence the expansion of a more intensive form of immigration policing, or what some analysts describe as 'territorial policing'. And aspects of it are subcontracted to the private sector, as in northern France, where the UK government, in September 2016, put out to tender an estimated £80 million contract to cover search and arrest operations previously carried out by the Home Office Border Force, at the Eurotunnel, Calais and Dunkirk. In its report, *Death at the Fences, Profits for Goldman Sachs*, Calais Research identifies the key role the Eurotunnel company, owned by international investment firms (Goldman Sachs owns a 15 per cent share), has played in the militarisation of the border. The report argues that Eurotunnel is where political, financial and military interests come together at the heart of the Calais border system. Border security is financed by the French and British government but outsourced to Eurotunnel, with huge sums handed over in recent years to fund a 300-strong private security army headed by a former Gendarmerie lieutenant colonel with thirty-three years' service in the French military, and to install an array of surveillance and security technologies.

Territorial policing of undesirables is not just about deterrence. It is also, as Andreas reminds us, a highly symbolic way of exercising authority and power, 'projecting an image of moral resolve' and thereby 'propping up the state's territorial authority'. In many countries, immigration law enforcement enjoys the support of the public, who internalise the government's 'insider–outsider' messages about foreign criminals and welfare scroungers and can even take voyeuristic pleasure (from the safety of their sofas) from the spectacle of enforcement (through Sky's Home Office–funded fly-on-the-wall TV documentary series 'UK Border Force', for instance). In the world of work, too, immigration enforcement plays a role beyond the obvious. Corporate Watch estimates that the Home Office carries out around 6,000 immigration workplace raids a year, making 5,000 arrests, around half of which lead to deportation.[7] But, given that undocumented workers are the 'base level of the driving sectors of the UK economy' (building workers, office cleaners, food pickers and packers, warehouse lifters, drivers and couriers), Corporate Watch questions the purpose of these raids, concluding that they are designed not to end illegal work, but to confine 'illegals' within a 'two-tier workforce' in which hundreds of thousands of workers have no access to the rights or safeguards available to other workers, and thus 'work more fearfully'.

Controversial immigration policing operations in other European countries have included Operation White Christmas (Italy), Operation Xenios Zeus (Greece) and Operation Reva (Sweden). Operation Reva Rule of Law and Effective Enforcement Work (Rättsäkert och Effektivt Verkställighetsarbete) was a nationwide operation across Sweden, funded largely by the EU and aimed at the pursuit, detention and deportation of undocumented migrants. Introduced following a shake-up of immigration enforcement, to give a greater role in removals to the National Police Board and the prison service, Operation Reva led to a marked increase in police presence on the streets of certain neighbourhoods, as well as on the metro and trams. Not surprisingly, it was deeply unpopular with young people of colour in Sweden, who quickly found themselves singled out for identity checks, leading to demonstrations against racial profiling in Malmö, Stockholm, Gothenburg, Norrköping and Uppsala.

But the expansion of immigration policing and its creep into everyday life are not confined to countries within the EU. According to Andreas, the EU has been able to 'thicken its borders by utilising neighbours as buffers'. This process, in relation to Africa, has been attacked as 'morally unacceptable' by Doctors Without Borders. In summer 2016, following the death in Mauritania of Malian migrant Mody Boubou Coulibaly, who jumped from a third-floor window after being chased by police, a number of African civil-society groups issued a joint statement condemning the 'hunting policies for migrants that grow everywhere on the African continent with the support of the European institutions under the guise of the fight against "irregular" migration'. The groups also pointed out that in Libya, a heavily armed 'anti-immigration brigade', with the support of the EU, 'tracks day and night the sub-Saharan migrant workers cram in detention centers' (sic).[8]

Meanwhile, in Europe, there is barely any judicial oversight of specialist squads such as the Brigada de Expulsiones de Delincuentes Extranjeros in Spain and the border defence guards of Hungary, which have swelled in numbers. A 47,000-strong border force operates not just in border areas but in several Hungarian cities; they are officially described as *határvadászok* ('border hunters') instead of *rendőrök* ('policemen'). Recruitment scouts visit secondary schools and promise wages far in excess of the usual wage for young people willing to do this work. As Eva S. Balogh, editor of hungarianspectrum.org, perceptively points out, naming 'these new border guards "border hunters" is significant. A guard is passive until whatever he is guarding is attacked. A hunter actively pursues the game.'[9]

Similarly, democratic oversight of Frontex, which also acts in so-called 'buffer countries', is sparse, and the campaigning organisation Frontexit points out that there is no independent mechanism in the mandate of the new border and coast

159

guard agency to hold it directly accountable at a judicial level. The International Organization for Migration (IOM), which started out as an inter-state body but is now part of the UN, is also generously funded by European countries, even as the EU reduces financial contributions to the UN High Commission for Refugees. In 2014, the IOM, for which a humanitarian mission ranks low in its priorities, had a budget of $1.3 billion and offices in more than 150 countries, with 480 field locations and 2,600 projects around the world.[10]

A Chain of Beneficiaries

Many profit when people are treated as commodities or units of exchange to be shifted like parcels, from one detention facility, accommodation centre, biometric security-guard-controlled container (as at Calais), or specially designated prison for foreign nationals, to the next. The chain of beneficiaries embraces multinational companies and their shareholders (bidding for government contracts), global banks and investment bankers (providing finance to build detention centres and prisons), private security companies like G4S (running detention centres and escort services), constructors of detention and processing centres and global management consultancy firms like McKinsey & Co., which helped the German government to implement more forceful deportation policies. And the beneficiaries are not only in Europe. In line with a strategy to control population movements as close to source as possible (the southern migration frontier of the EU has been progressively externalised), the EU is constructing immigration detention centres in West Africa, and even entering into agreements with the pariah states of Sudan and Eritrea, ensuring that the EU not only attempts to control entries to its own territory, but also movements within the African continent. A variety of other measures are also deployed to browbeat countries around the Mediterranean, and as far afield as sub-Saharan Africa, to undertake immigration controls on the EU's behalf, as well as take back refugees. In October 2016, the EU signed an agreement with Afghanistan according to which around 200,000 Afghans would be returned to a country in the grip of an intensifying war in exchange for €1 billion a year in aid, with a further $5 billion to follow in military aid and the promise of the construction of a new terminal at Kabul's airport specifically designed for migrants rejected by EU member-states.[11]

The promise to build new processing centres is not confined to refugees, but extends to 'problematic' resident non-EU populations within Europe. The UK, for instance, has funded a reception centre at Lagos's Murtala Muhammed International Airport, for processing people forcibly returned to Nigeria by UK immigration,[12] and has announced that it will spend £25 million on building a prison in Jamaica so that those of Jamaican citizenship, even if brought up in the UK, can be sent 'home' to serve sentences in the Caribbean. Germany's federal migration and refugee office, according to leaked documents, proposes to build orphanages for deported minors in Morocco; and the Belgian state, having refused to protect its own national Ali Aarrass, extradited by Spain to the Moroccan torture-state, has since 2012 sent dozens of Moroccan nationals 'back' to serve prison sentences in Morocco. In 2013 the leader of the New Flemish Alliance Party said Belgium should fund a prison there, since 'there are 1,200 Moroccans behind bars in Belgium, enough to fill a prison in Morocco'.

On any asylum market league table of profit-driven innovation, border and surveillance technology manufacturers would be right at the top. This is a sought-after area for scientific research, and new advances are swiftly being transferred to other areas of social control. Frontex itself has been a beneficiary of the Copernicus programme, a European system for monitoring the earth that comprises a complex set of systems collecting data from multiple sources: earth-observation satellites, ground stations, and airborne, seaborne and other sensors. Refugee advocates have pointed out time and again that those specialising in border technology have a vested interest in con-juring up threats, as the more menacing and diffuse the risk at the border appears, the greater the need for innovation and the higher the profit. The 'illegality industry' is how Ruben Anders-son refers to this, pointing out that border technology 'creates what it is meant to eliminate or transform' – namely, 'more migrant illegality'.[13]

The market for border control is endless: it embraces the construction and perimeter-protection industries, fingerprint processing, facial recognition and other surveillance, and inspection and detection technologies (satellite, radar, thermo-graphic cameras, drones, carbon dioxide sensors, mechanical sniffer dogs), as well as the so-called 'less lethal' weapons of crowd control (tear gas and plastic bullets are fast becoming the norm for crowd control at borders). Watchtowers also need to be built, and, according to boundary experts, Europe is on the verge of having as many security fences and border walls between countries as it did during the Cold War. This is all part of an international trend. Since the fall of the Berlin Wall, over forty countries around the world have built fences against more than sixty of their neighbours, with the majority citing security concerns and the prevention of illegal migration as justification.[14] Andreas predicts that future innovation will be in the field of 'virtual fencing'. Based on non-lethal microwave technology developed by the Pentagon, it creates a burning sensation without actually burning the skin. He also predicts the use of video-equipped (and potentially armed) unmanned dirigibles and robots in border-control duties.

Many other institutional stakeholders profit further down the asylum market's complex chain. The market needs its analysts and experts, border and perimeter specialists, migra-tion mappers and risk assessors. Jobs are created in language analysis and special forensic services (DNA analysis for family reunification claims, age assessments), training and consul-tancy (training African countries in border management, for instance).

Migratory movements also bring opportunities for the new 'venture philanthropists' (who borrow their language and methods from venture capital) and 'compassionate capitalists', who promise to harness the creative spirit and technological ingenuity of capitalism for the benefit of migrants and refugees.[15] Thus, digital technology companies provide new multilingual and asylum information apps for refugees, special sim cards for migrants (designed by the likes of Vodafone) and blockchain-powered infrastructures to facilitate digital identification. Then there is Western Union, reaping fees for migrant transactions, and, even further down the chain (and in ways that may yet shape human relationships for the good), the local shopkeepers who adapt their products to cater for the refugees and migrants. On the Greek islands, for instance, stores that used to focus on tourists now sell tents, sleeping bags and food to boat people, and hotels offer discounts to migrants outside the tourist season.

Finally, there are the international aid agencies and Third Sector organisations that have been integrated into neoliberal norms of governance via the outsourcing of key state responsibilities to networks drawn from a nexus of private, state, and Third Sector actors. Not all of these groups are co-opted wholesale into the asylum market through their partnerships with government and global security companies that subcontract them as service providers. Some manage to hold to their humanitarian ethos, bringing hope, friendship and a reminder of 'European decency' to migrants and refugees. But, as Lydie Arbogast warns, NGOs and humanitarian organisations need to ensure that, by their actions, they do not contribute to the 'normalisation of detention measures where infringements of fundamental rights are inherent'.[16]

Chancellor Merkel's decision to suspend the Dublin regulation and open up a safe passage into Germany for Syrian refugees in the summer of 2015 bucked the trend. But once the dangerous bottleneck of refugees threatening to overwhelm Europe's capacities to manage migration was cleared, the neoliberal EU returned to doing what it does best: abandoning refugees to the beggar-your-neighbour policies of the member-states.

Structured Violence: Demonisation, Distanciation, Authorisation

In September 2015, the European Commission promised to deliver a policy of cooperation and resettlement through the mandatory dispersal of 160,000 refugees from Greece and Italy throughout the EU. One year later, fewer than 6,000 people had been relocated (3.75 per cent). In the face of member-state intransigence, the EU has not only abandoned its responsibility for the thousands of refugees stranded in Europe, it has also presided over conditions of structured violence. To manage and cover up the nature of the system it oversees, along with member-states, it has utilised the practices and techniques described by Australian academics Leanne Weber and Sharon Pickering. These include: distanciation, in which complex chains of responsibility make it difficult to connect causes (such as government policies) with effects (such as border-related deaths); deliberate strategies of demonisation and neutralisation, which represent the targets of harmful policies as threatening and undeserving; and deeply ingrained patterns of authorisation, whereby large sections of the population can be persuaded to accept even the most egregious acts, if they are portrayed as necessary in order to achieve some higher goal, such as orderly borders and the protection of national security.[17]

The EU turns a blind eye, as the border and coastguard agency it bankrolls is complicit in injury and death at the Greek maritime border. Internal, unredacted Frontex reports obtained by the *Intercept* show that European coastguards' rules of engagement sanction shooting at boats crewed by suspected smugglers *irrespective* of whether refugees are injured or killed in the process. This unearthed truth about the deviant nature of Frontex should come as no surprise, since both the Spanish Civil Guard (at Ceuta and Melilla), and Hungarian and Bulgarian border guards have been implicated in the deaths of refugees. Fifteen migrants drowned in February 2014 when Spanish civil guards used rubber bullets and smoke canisters to stop them swimming round a seawall dividing Morocco from the Spanish enclave of Ceuta at El Tarajal. But an investigation into sixteen members of the civil guard was discontinued after a judge ruled that their actions were legitimate. And when, in June 2016, Syrian refugee Farhan al-Hwaish drowned in Hungary in a branch of the Tisza river which forms the border with Serbia, police denied any involvement, although, according to al-Hwaish's brother, police threw objects at a group of refugees as they swam, sprayed them with gas and released attack dogs on them when they attempted to climb out of the water. Hungarian prosecutors opened an investigation in June 2016 to see whether any officers could be held criminally responsible, but the investigation was soon closed down. In February 2017, another refugee, Rahmat Ullah Hanife, drowned in the same river. Eye witnesses say that police laughed and joked as he fell through the cracked ice.

State violence at the border is now the norm, as is the constant persecution by the state (and by non-state actors – see Chapter 4) of those living in makeshift refugee camps, like the 'Jungle' in Calais (until its demolition in November 2016) or those that spring up in the borderlands, where 'invisible refugees' hide out in abandoned buildings and in forests. Here, particularly at the Hungarian borders with Bulgaria and Serbia, migrants are vulnerable to the murderous activities of vigilantes and 'hunting parties'. There must be no 'no-man's land' where legal norms do not apply, warn Human Rights Watch (HRW) and Hungary's Migrant Solidarity Group (Migszol), both of which have documented crimes committed by Hungarian soldiers and a local authority civil militia (so-called field guards), who beat refugees with batons and fists, set dogs on them, and used sprays that caused burning sensations to the eyes as well as plastic handcuffs causing further injuries.[18] Physical beatings have also been meted out by Hungarian and Bulgarian military guards in government-controlled camps, and HRW has called for some members of the Bulgarian police and military to be prosecuted for robbery, as they have been stripping migrants and refugees of their possessions before dumping them at the Turkish border. In summer 2016, the Bar Human Rights Committee of England and Wales was among organisations calling for an investigation into violence by police and gendarmes (a military force charged with police duties) at Calais and Dunkirk, where the French CRC riot police were accused of excessive use of tear gas and of beating migrants with batons, sticks and truncheons. In one documented incident, a sixteen-year-old Iranian was among those forced to kneel down in a line before being repeatedly beaten with truncheons in a field outside Calais. In Greece, such techniques have also been used against unaccompanied children in police stations. Twelve minors of Pakistani origin were transferred from the Moria reception centre to a police detention centre in Mytilene, where they were held for around twenty-three hours, most of the time in a kneeling position; when they moved, the officers hit them with water bottles.

At the eleven 'hotspots' that the EU has created in the 'frontline countries' of Italy and Greece to swiftly screen, interrogate and fingerprint incoming migrants, not only are conditions unsanitary and food inadequate, but on the Greek island of Chios babies have been starved through inadequate supplies of milk formula. The downgrading of humanitarianism is in line with the hotspots' raison d'être – namely, with Europol cooperation, to gather intelligence on and from each migrant from the outset. Military-run camps on the Greek–Macedonian border have been described by volunteer workers as 'filthy, derelict warehouses … not fit for animals'.[19] Of thirteen preventable refugee and migrant deaths that occurred in Greece from April 2016 to January 2017, six occurred in the hotspots, five at Moria, Lesbos. Carbon monoxide poisoning from dangerous heaters was the cause of most of these deaths, though autopsy results are shrouded in secrecy.

The Violence of Privatisation

The *Guardian*'s publication of the Nauru files drew attention to the state violence in Australia's system of privatised, offshore detention centres on the remote Pacific Islands of Nauru and Manus Island (Papua New Guinea).[20] These have been run since 2014 by Broadspectrum (formerly Transfield), which in May 2016 was taken over by the Spanish company Ferrovial SA.[21] In Europe, national responsibilities for asylum detention tend to obscure the fact that, just as in Australia, it is the international, integrated system of migration management that produces human rights abuses, irrespective of national variations. What happens in Europe broadly follows the same pattern as Australia, as both continents are part of an integrated system of global migration control within the 'neoliberal abandonment' paradigm. Anyone in doubt need only examine a string of revelations about the practices of Frontex, the military and the police. As in Australia (where Ferrovial's predecessors G4S and Broadspectrum face a lawsuit alleging human rights violations), private security companies have figured prominently in human rights scandals. In the UK, G4S has faced multiple accusations of racist and sexist abuse in immigration removal centres.[22] An inquest has returned a verdict of unlawful killing on the death of Jimmy Mubenga, an Angolan deportee who died of a heart attack in 2010 under restraint by three of its employees during a deportation flight (although the three were later acquitted of his manslaughter). Meanwhile, in Australia, G4S lost its contract to run the Nauru detention centre after repeated allegations of sexual assault and torture and a government inquiry into the death of Iranian refugee Reza Berati. Fifteen G4S employees were implicated in the killing of Berati, who was beaten to death, one G4S guard (later convicted of murder) having dropped a large rock on his head. In Europe, other private security companies at the centre of critical publicity include Hoppetgruppen (Sweden), PeWoBe, Siba security service GmbH and European Homecare (Germany). Some of the most serious cases involve European Homecare. Images emerged in late 2014 of a security guard at a refugee welcome centre in Burbach standing on the head of an asylum seeker. In another image, a man was forced to lie on a mattress covered in his own vomit. The North Rhine-Westphalia state prosecutor now has a 50,000-page file detailing alleged offences in accommodation centres run by European Homecare, including accusations against both management and security guards.

Crucially, criticism of private security companies is not confined to the containment market. Just as international organisations for migration control (such as Frontex and the IOM) cleverly market themselves in humanitarian terms, so too do the private security companies that have moved into the care market. But, as the European Homecare example shows only too clearly, punishment, not care, is intrinsic to ruthless cost-cutting and profit-driven exercises. Seeking accountability for such structured violence is hard, as private providers outsource services to smaller companies; within such a complex web of responsibility, as Weber and Pickering pointed out, it is doubly difficult to connect cause with effect. G4S's system of multi-subcontracting to accommodation providers on the basis of three or four tiers of landlords, each one slicing off a share of the profit, has been described as hopelessly inefficient; the company has faced multi-million-pound fines from the UK Home Office for its extremely poor performance as an accommodation provider.

The record of Swedish providers, too, is questionable. Sweden takes more unaccompanied minors than any other European country, but private sector involvement in their care may put them at risk. Aleris, Jokarjo and Hoppetgruppen have all been accused of reaping maximum profits from their treatment of unaccompanied children, through overcharging, understaffing and the provision of poor-quality accommodation and food. Since accommodating minors is far more lucrative than accommodating adults, suppliers with any kind of accommodation, even caravans or dormitories that can sleep fifteen, have submitted tenders. When Alexandra Mezher, a twenty-two-year-old social worker of Lebanese origin, was stabbed to death in January 2016 by a young Ethiopian with mental health problems at a refugee centre in Mölndal, near Gothenburg, the cost-cutting activities of HVB Living Nordic, a private company paid £22.6 million by the local authority to provide housing and care for unaccompanied minors, became a hot issue. Mezher had been called in to cover a night shift, and was supervising eleven inmates on her own. Sweden's Work Environment Administration has initiated an investigation into suspected occupational health and safety violations, but most of the outrage is now directed at Mezher's killer, because it emerged at his trial that he was several years older than initially thought, and was not a minor.

John Grayson, a campaigner with the South Yorkshire Migration and Asylum Action Group in the UK, has done much to prise open the activities of private companies that subcontract to other companies and hide behind outsourcing when they are named and shamed.[23] When, following yet more scandals, the Home Office launched an investigation into its asylum housing contract with G4S for the north-east of England, the company was investigated by the *Times*. The paper discovered that the accommodation provision had been subcontracted to Jomast, whose owner, Stuart Monk, had a fortune estimated at £175 million. Likewise, Serco, at the centre of a BBC and *Times* investigation alleging that it accommodated asylum seekers in 'dirty, dangerous and cockroach-infested homes', where residents were intimidated, sexually harassed and bullied, could point to the fact that the subcontracted provider was Orchard & Shipman.[24] In a case from Germany, Pond Security, which had a contract to provide security at asylum reception centres in Hessen, subcontracted services at a centre in Calden to another company, Spectra Security. The trade union ver.di blames excessive subcontracting for poor conditions at the centre, alleging vicious treatment of staff, many of whom do not speak German. One former employee is suing the company for withholding salaries, and for imposing impossible working conditions and weeks of twelve-hour shifts without breaks. In February 2016, a security guard at the centre was shot dead, and another guard was arrested for the killing.[25]

This ruthless profit-driven decision-making, intrinsic to outsourced systems, ensures that, despite the efforts of activists like John Grayson, accountability and justice for asylum seekers are virtually impossible to achieve. Corralled within a system that has, at least since the 1990s, been characterised by xeno-racism, the reification, dehumanisation and structural racism practised against those that the Australian indigenous critic Tony Birch refers to as the 'unpeopled' intensifies in privatised systems.

The Design and Logistics of Xeno-Racism

Today, architects and designers in France are the latest to be accused – by their peers – of complicity in xeno-racist policies that turn people into human cargo and disposable objects. The French Socialist government, which first demolished the southern part of the vast shanty-town at Calais known as the Jungle, before forcibly evicting those who remained, stands accused of 'abandoning people fleeing war-torn countries' and, as a consequence, 're-traumatizing them by deploying more force and violence'.[26] The French government's offer to some of those it has uprooted? Around 125 shipping containers, transformed into living units with the capacity to accommodate 1,500 people, who can only gain access via biometric scan. (Each migrant is numbered, like the containers.) In an op-ed in *Libération* ('A Camp From the 1930s in Calais'), architect Cyrille Hanappe described a system that treats people as objects and denies individual identity as an affront to human dignity.[27] Not so, said the Socialists, who marketed it as state-of-the-art 'humanitarian accommodation' generously financed by the government to the tune of €18 million.

The design of the Calais humanitarian container camp brought about yet another convergence – between military logistics, architects and designers – in an extension of xeno-racism. 'Architecture and design are instruments of domination' providing 'the spatial and territorial conditions for racism to exercise itself', argues Léopold Lambert, editor of the *Funambulist*, in his introduction to a special issue of the magazine on design and racism, which includes an essay on 'Container Politics in the Jungle' by anthropologist Miriam Ticktin.[28] The company given the Calais contract (under an opaque tendering system) is Brittany-based Logistic Solutions, whose founder, Norbert Janvier, worked until 2006 in French military intelligence. Logistic Solutions counts the French army among its major clients.[29] Such companies are now leading providers of accommodation, as the building of 'humanitarian infrastructures' is outsourced to technology, logistics and military concerns. To paraphrase Lambert and Ticktin, these containers force a particular way of being on their inhabitants, 'reordering the boundaries of the human', turning those stowed away into 'an inferior kind of human' – a thing, to be packaged and lodged in metal reservations on the edges of Europe.

But under systems of neoliberal governance, ever more vulnerable groups, and not just asylum seekers and refugees, are being 'unpeopled'. Witness the neoliberal abandonment, from the 1990s onwards, of people with mental health or addiction problems to incarceration within an ever-expanding penal state. The prison population in the UK – the highest in Europe – is expanding each year, due also to continually increasing sentences and the growing use of indeterminate, extended and life sentences with no fixed prison term attached. This has been compounded by the impact on the poor of the joint enterprise laws (otherwise known as common purpose) which allow for multiple convictions of young people (disproportionately BAME communities, refugees and 'virtual nationals'), allowing the police and prosecution service to scoop up young people at the scene of a knife crime and charge them all with murder, irrespective of whether they wielded the knife – or, indeed, whether they had any contact with the victim at all. The Howard League for Penal Reform is among those drawing attention to the unprecedented epidemic of poor mental health currently being experienced in British prisons. In 2016, one suicide occurred every three days – the highest death toll in a calendar year since records began, in 1978. That is always the lesson gleaned from any system of racism. Once systems have been put in place for one category of people, they can easily be applied to another. As Angela Davis noted, in a different context, 'If they come for me in the morning, they will come for you at night.' This leads us to a final question: How can we build solidarity and resistance in the face of the authoritarian solutions of nationalists, neoliberals and the hard right?

8

'They Shall Not Pass'

Neoliberal elites, having once extolled the virtues of the global village, are responding to the nationalist challenge by packaging globalisation in a more patriotic and authoritarian wrapper. In fact, authoritarian solutions have always been an aspect of neoliberalism, and there is much in its practice (as opposed to its superficial ideology) that nationalists can build on. Punishment of the weak and vulnerable is as intrinsic to neoliberalism in the UK as it is to authoritarian nationalism in Hungary. Neoliberalism and authoritarianism have been wedded, too, in the workplace. Workfare, labour deregulation, zero-hour contracts, unwillingness to enforce the minimum wage, the bullying of workers – all these forms of autocratic management would have been impossible without a boundary-marking national political culture and a divide-and-rule politics wherein the citizen-worker and the rightless migrant are clearly delineated. The most insecure category of workers in Europe today are migrant workers. This is clear from the number of cases in the UK involving household-name retailers like Boots, BHS and Sports Direct, manufacturing companies such as Hawkeswood Metal Recycling and agricultural gangmasters like DJ Houghton Chicken Catching Services.[1] The treatment of such migrant and, indeed, other precarious workers is facing mounting legal and moral challenges. An undercover investigation by the *Guardian* forced through changes at Sports Direct, where warehouse staff, mostly eastern Europeans, were required to go through searches at the end of each shift, and also suffered deductions from their wages for clocking in for a shift just one minute late, taking their pay below the minimum wage.[2] In a landmark ruling, DJ Houghton Chicken Catching Services became the first British company to be liable under legislation on modern slavery, and was ordered to compensate six Lithuanian men for the severe exploitation they had suffered after being trafficked into the UK.[3]

Legal challenges like this, and the public exposure they generate, are important; nevertheless, the law has been weak in protecting us from the hollowing-out of democracy that neoliberalism has engendered. Not just an economic project, neoliberalism is deeply political – an attempt to transform the state from within, merging nation-states into interconnecting market-states. To date, the EU supranational entity, with its weak parliament and unaccountable European Commission, has been central to that process. By subordinating 'social Europe' (social protection and equality) to the interests of global corporations and global finance (competition law and market efficiencies), those who drive the European Commission may have created the conditions for the EU's nemesis – nationalism – and, following Brexit, for potential dissolution, though firm predictions are not yet possible.

Paradoxically, nationalism may yet prove highly advantageous to multinational corporations and neoliberal transnational forces. In grossly unequal and socially volatile societies that are increasingly rejecting austerity in favour of protectionism or socialism, only a more commanding and authoritarian state can finalise the transition from nation- to market-state. If nationalism can be tamed, its merit for supranational elites is that it could well deliver a more regimented national community. If the market-state is to continue to advance the interests of global finance in an economically diminished and socially divided

Europe, then national elites, whose responsibility it is to ensure a stable environment for global capital, must set clear limits. Inequality, in the final analysis, demands to be policed. In the market-state, the state serves not the nation but transnational capital. The state, therefore, must turn enabler, unfettering the market to ensure the best conditions for transnational capital to operate, and thereby – as neoliberal myth would have it – maximising the opportunities enjoyed by all members of society.[4] The neoliberal enabler-state may still be necessary economically. But, for political reasons, the state must turn enforcer, guaranteeing that social disorder does not threaten political order. Nationalism might well provide the route into the 'strong state', albeit that the stability that transnational capitalism seeks to create differs from its nineteenth-century counterpart. A modern 'strong state' does not need state terror when it has in its arsenal the total control brought about by the revolution in biometric and digital technologies. A shrinking state in terms of welfare, but an expanded, centralised and total state in the realms of social control, discipline and power.

Nationalism, nativism, the military ethos, the setting of boundaries between citizen and migrant, the promise of national security in the face of the Muslim enemy within – all are means to an end, ensuring that the public colludes in policing itself within the technological security apparatus that has grown up alongside the market-state. In this sense, nationalism, far from representing a break with neoliberalism, provides the climate that allows for its break from democracy.

The Centrality of Anti-Fascism

But the turf war between global neoliberals and nationalists does not have a predetermined outcome. If authoritarian ideas are deeply rooted in European culture, so too are humanitarian, anti-fascist and socialist ones. Indeed, I have been at pains in this book to draw attention to the transformations already taking place on the left. Though the circumstances are different today from those of the 1930s, anti-fascism can still serve as metaphor, conceptual framework and key to opening up spaces for struggle. The slogan most associated with the anti-fascist cause – 'No pasarán!' – is, in its broadest sense, a passionate encapsulation of the interdependent relationship between the fight for humanity and the defence of democracy. Today's socialism, like anti-fascism, must defend cultural pluralism, a basic tenet of democracy. The hard right is trying to undermine cultural pluralism, manipulating referendums, and using direct democracy to assert the tyranny of the majority, undermine the human rights of immigrants and attack the civil rights (including religious rights) of vulnerable minorities. Democratic renewal needs its tribunes and its electoral parties; without them, the authoritarian right will remain in power. But political parties can no longer challenge the extreme right through centralised machine politics, media and spin. The left must be rooted in local communities, supporting new models of economic and community regeneration based on self-help to give people hope and dignity. Neoliberalism has taken away that dignity, and if the left does not address that, the ultra-right will – offering the catharsis of violence.

In any cultural revolution from the left, anti-racism, too, cannot be reduced to identity politics or manipulated by political interests, as we have seen when definitions of anti-Semitism are hijacked, but has to be embedded in community struggles. It is here, at the local level, where the ultra-right attempts to advance like an invasive weed, that anti-fascism is at its most vibrant and potent, refashioned as it is by a fresh generation of young people who are discovering the importance of anti-fascism anew. Supporting local communities of resistance as they struggle against violence, whether it be from the far right or the police, is the best protection against the narrow perspectives of the policy-orientated 'hate crime' industry, which strays too close to government, emptying anti-racism of its progressive content and allowing politicians and the media to reduce a political struggle to a vacuous fairy tale about challenging bad people who use nasty words.

In challenging what Sivanandan describes as the 'market state', with its 'market morality' and racist popular culture, its 'social stereotypes' and 'anti-scrounger', 'anti-immigrant patriotism',[5] values based on community and solidarity must come to the fore, as should a recognition that unity in diversity makes a community stronger. Anti-fascism, then – in its broadest sense – has got to be at the heart of socialist pluralism and left-wing cultural democratic renewal, which also embraces all that is best in the European humanitarian tradition. Reading far-right websites like Breitbart News, which constantly features stories of humanitarians who fall victim to 'immigrant crimes', brings awareness of just how hated humanitarians (seen as 'race traitors') are by the far right. The humanitarian approach to human life and human dignity is the exact opposite of that of fascists. In the run-up to the Holocaust, Hitler's academics coined the term *Lebensunwertes Leben* ('life unworthy of life') to denote those sections of the populace (at first, the mentally and physically disabled) who had no right to live. Although, of course, there were no state-sanctioned euthanasia programmes today, as there was under Nazism, those abandoned by neo-liberalism – the mentally ill, the disabled, the incarcerated, the unemployed, the poor, the elderly – have effectively been categorised as 'disposable' people.

Anti-fascism is not just about mobilising against the fascists, important as that is. As Greek anti-fascists on the frontline of resistance today have argued, 'anti-fascism is a political struggle about the kind of life we want to live in ... it is a battle for democracy, solidarity and social justice'.[6] For those who support refugees and oppose the building of more walls and razor fences, the mission must be to reinsert into the vocabulary of anti-fascism an understanding of the relationship between fascism, war, militarism and securitisation. Just as in previous generations conscientious objectors refused military service, today's humanitarians are the new dissenters, objecting to laws and practices that treat refugees as 'life unworthy of life'. Dozens of people across Europe are being prosecuted for what have come to be known as 'crimes of solidarity', yet the European Commission is refusing to review its laws on facilitation of entry to Europe, which treat those who are motivated by humanitarian instincts as akin to traffickers. Those prosecuted include the Danish children's writer and campaigner Lisbeth Zornig, arrested in March 2016 for giving a family of Syrian refugees coffee and a lift; French farmer Cedric Herrou, given a suspended fine of €3,000 in February 2007 for helping African refugees enter France; French activist Felix Croft, arrested in Italy for giving a lift to a refugee family into France; and interpreter Francesca Peirotti, arrested in France for a similar offence. In addition, three Spanish firefighters who volunteered as lifeguards in the Mediterranean for Professional Emergency Aid have been charged with attempted human trafficking and weapons offences for the possession of a rope knife – a mandatory element of the rescue kit.

Thirdly, and relatedly, socialist values and democratic renewal must be linked in a challenge – both intellectual and material – to bureaucratic practices that, by their very essence, destroy the integrity of the individual. In the previous century, two Jewish scholars, Hannah Arendt and Zygmunt Bauman, in *Eichmann in Jerusalem: A Report on the Banality of Evil* and *Modernity and the Holocaust*, respectively, set out to understand the social, political and economic factors that led to the Holocaust. Both scholars linked Hitler's crimes, particularly the Final Solution, to the rise of modern bureaucracies that seek optimal solutions, subordinating thought and action to pragmatism and efficiency, reducing individuals to functionaries of a bureaucratic hierarchy, so that officials, conditioned to follow orders, lose the ability to function and think as moral individuals. There are clear parallels with what is happening today, under conditions of neoliberal governance. In the field of asylum and immigration, for instance, inhumane systems are put in place by functionaries, with some Third Sector organisations that have become integrated into the process losing their moral compass.

A Public Record of State Violence

At the Institute of Race Relations in London, we have been documenting the structural violence of Europe's asylum and immigration bureaucracies, as well as the criminal justice system's biased treatment of people of colour in the UK and Europe. As part of the European Research Programme, we try to keep a record of all those 'foreigners' who have died either in Europe's immigration and removal centres, destitute on the streets, or by their own hands, having despaired of ever reaching safety or receiving justice. In relation to the UK, my colleagues Harmit Athwal and Jenny Bourne, who co-authored *Dying for Justice*, have found that 509 people from BAME, refugee and migrant communities died between 1991 and 2014 in suspicious circumstances in which the police, prison authorities or immigration detention officers were implicated.

What we have attempted to create, then, is a public record of state violence – one that throws a spotlight on the practices and logic of state institutions. It is an archive that could not exist without counting the dead. 'Counting', according to Australian scholars Leanne Weber and Sharon Pickering, 'is about finding a "trace of life" that can be recorded, and this trace reveals the structural violence of the state'.[7] When it comes to an individual's choice to end their own life, the authorities reduce suicide to psychological factors, they write. 'Complex chains of causation are absented, and the context of the hopelessness of detention is thereby erased.'

What more can we do, both at Europe's external and internal borders, to ensure that counting and archiving translates into something more profound, including the active protection of human life and dignity? Groups like Amnesty International,

Human Rights Watch and the Council of Europe are constantly issuing press releases and urgent action alerts, reminding governments of their responsibilities under international law. But perhaps it is time to go beyond such denunciations and exhortations, and look at proactive legal interventions. There is a legal term, 'depraved indifference', which refers to conduct that is so wanton, so callous, so reckless, so morally lacking in concern and regard for the lives of others, and thus so blameworthy, as to warrant criminal liability. Surely Europe's approach to asylum and migrants now constitutes a case of 'depraved indifference'?

The Destruction of Empathy

But it is not just what we are doing to migrants, asylum seekers and those without papers that should be linked to the legal concept of 'depraved indifference' or the Nazi doctrine of 'life unworthy of life'. Certain categories of people can only be treated as unworthy of consideration if the wider culture of society actively permits it by destroying empathy for the other. A market-driven and celebrity-orientated popular culture, by encouraging consumerism and envy, drives us away from values based on collectivity, intellectual curiosity (about the interconnectedness of the world, and hence the reasons for refugee flight) and empathy for the other. The way in which 'outsiders', whether they be refugees, Muslims, or Roma, the working poor or the unemployed, are demonised and dehumanised by politicians, the media and other sections of society – and not only the extreme right – has created a hostile, racist climate in which those of us who try to fight for a Europe underpinned by humanitarian values are derided as weak-minded and unpatriotic. It is a Europe where the whistle-blowers who act out of conscience to expose corruption and state violence are quickly excommunicated, turned into outsiders and outlaws.

Broad-based alliances are already being created against a culture that begins to resemble fascism. Filmmakers, performance artists, dramatists and visual artists are taking the raw material of campaigners and amplifying the data of activists, so that the truth of Europe's appalling treatment of the vulnerable and the marginalised becomes a 'revelation that must be heard'.[8] Certainly, we face a great challenge – namely, the moral ambiguity of large sections of society; the challenge of non-listening, non-seeing, non-feeling. To be seen and heard, we need a vocabulary, a syntax to shock people out of complacency. There is much in the language of past struggles that we can draw upon. 'They Shall Not Pass' is not an indication of the left's 'extremism'; it is the measure of just how much we value democracy.

Notes

Introduction

1. See M. McGovern, 'Inquiring into Collusion? Collusion, the State and the Management of Truth Recovery in Northern Ireland', *State Crime Journal* 2: 1 (2013); and 'State Violence and the Colonial Roots of Collusion in Northern Ireland', *Race & Class* 57: 2 (2015).
2. From the official definition of collusion that came out of the 2004 Cory Inquiry into the murder of the human rights lawyer Pat Finucane.

1. Preparing for Race War

1. See S. Bangstad, *Anders Breivik and the Rise of Islamophobia* (London: Zed, 2014).
2. The point about the deceptive nature of the far right's embrace of philozionism is made forcefully by the writer and broadcaster Anne Karpf, who argues, in 'Don't Be Fooled: Europe's Far-Right Racists Are Not Discerning' (*Guardian*, 28 March 2012) that both the philozionist and the anti-Semite see 'the Jew' as a 'unified racial category. Beneath the admiring surface, philozionism isn't really an appreciation of Jewish culture but

rather the opportunistic endorsement of Israeli nationalism and power.'

3. For the most complete account of the infiltration of the Greek police and military, see D. Christopoulos, ed., *Mapping Ultra-Right Extremism and Xenophobia and Racism Within the Greek State Apparatus* (Brussels: Rosa Luxemburg Stiftung, 2014). See also FIDH and Hellenic League for Human Rights, *Downgrading Human Rights: The Cost of Austerity in Greece* (Paris: FIDH, 2014).

4. Alain Soral founded Réconciliation in France, and in Belgium Laurent Louis heads up Debout Les Belges. Soral, once a member of the French Communist Party, later joined the Front National, which he left in 2000. Jean-Marie Le Pen is godfather to Dieudonné's son.

5. Gwendolyn Albert, who works with Roma, says that since about 2006 it has become standard for the media to use the term 'inadaptable' as a way of referring to the Roma, and the Czech News Agency issues press releases without even bothering to put quotation marks around the term. See also M. Šimůnková, 'Czech Govt Human Rights Commissioner: The Term "Inadaptable" Deprives Roma of Their Humanity', 19 May 2013, at romea.cz.

6. University of Bielefeld, *Rechtsextreme Strutkturen: Gruppenbezogene, Menschenfeindlichkeit und bürgerschaftliches Engagement gegen Rechtsextremisus in der Landeshauptstadt Dresden* (Bielefeld, 2011), p. 15, Table 7; p. 106, Table 8.

7. A. Fano Fernandez, 'Germany's New Far Right', *Jacobin*, 20 February 2015.

8. See J. Burnett, *Racial Violence and the Brexit State* (London: Institute of Race Relations, 2016).

9. B. Mauk, 'Diary', *London Review of Books*, 22 September 2016.

10. The Freital Group, which emerged from anti-migrant vigilante movements, is linked to a number of attacks on refugee accommodation, left-wing centres and politicians. Intelligence services acknowledged that explosives were used in two cases, and also drew attention to the group's links to the local branch of Pegida (Fregida). Amid disquiet about soft-peddling

by the local prosecutor's office and allegations not only that the Saxony police knew about the group and failed to intervene, but that at least one police officer tipped off its members about police operations, the federal prosecutors took over the investigation. Eight members of the Freital group were subsequently arrested on suspicion of forming a terrorist group. See J. Kushner, '10 Murders, 3 Nazis, and Germany's Moment of Reckoning', *Foreign Policy*, March 2017.

11. Bar Human Rights Committee of England and Wales, *Camps at Calais and Grand-Synthe (France): Policing and Access to Justice* (London, July 2016).

2. Understanding the Extreme Right

1. Alemmano started his journey as a youth leader with the neofascist Italian Socialist Movement, the party set up after the Second World War by the followers of Mussolini. He ran for mayor in 2008 under the flag of Silvio Berlusconi's Pole of Freedom.

2. The Swiss People's Party, while rooted in the country's conservative tradition, is a hybrid radical right-wing populist movement, in that since the 1990s, under the leadership of the millionaire Christoph Blocher, it has moved into extreme-right territory. It does not shrink from using racist language and imagery in its propaganda.

3. For a comparison with the United States, see W. Robinson and M. Barrera, 'Global Capitalism and Twenty-First Century Fascism: A US Case Study', *Race & Class* 53: 3 (2012).

4. P. Komaromi, 'Germany: Neo-Nazis and the Market in Asylum Reception', *Race & Class* 58: 2 (2015).

5. For the UK, see H. Athwal and J. Bourne, *Dying for Justice* (London: Institute of Race Relations, 2014). For France, see Collectif Angles Morts, *Permis de Tuer: chronique de l'impunité policière* (Paris: Editions Syllepse, 2014). And for Germany, see E. Bruce-Jones, 'German Policing at the Intersection: Race, Gender, Migrant Status and Mental Health', *Race & Class* 56: 3 (2015).

6. Both officers, who had a reputation for extreme policing methods and violence, were in fact sacked. Johan Demol was the police commissioner of Schaerbeek, Brussels, but was sacked in 1998 after his membership of the fascist militia, the Front de la Jeunesse, became known. (He went on to represent the Vlaams Blok/Belang, before finally being expelled in 2010.) Bart Debie, who now claims that between 2007 and 2010 he was employed by the security services to spy on the Vlaams Belang, was elected as a Vlaams Belang councillor in Antwerp in 2006, and had also acted as security advisor and spokesperson for the leader, Felip Dewinter, before being expelled in 2010.

7. The term was coined by Robert Warren. Cited in S. Graham, *Cities Under Siege: The New Military Urbanism* (London/ New York: Verso, 2011), p. 23.

8. N. Davies, 'The Bloody Battle of Genoa', *Guardian*, 17 July 2008. In April 2015, in a case brought by Arnaldo Cestaro, the European Court of Human Rights found Italy guilty of contravening Article 3 of the European Convention on Human Rights, which forbids torture and inhuman or degrading treatment, in relation to incidents at the Diaz-Pertini school, which had been made available as a site for demonstrators to sleep in by the city council. *Cestaro v Italy*, application 6884/11, ECtHR, 7 April 2015.

9. M. Margaronis, 'Greek Anti-Fascist Protestors "Tortured by Police" after Golden Dawn Clash', *Guardian*, 9 October 2012.

10. Amnesty International, *Spain: The Right to Protest Under Threat*, AI, 2014 (EUR 41/001/2014).

11. C. Froio and P. Castelli Gattinara, 'Neo-Fascist Mobilisation in Contemporary Italy: Ideology and Repertoire of Action of CasaPound Italia', *Journal for Deradicalisation* 2 (2015).

12. See A. Schmidt, *Völkische Siedler/inner im ländlichen Raum: Basiswissen und Handlungstrategien* (Berlin: Amadeu Antonio Foundation, 2015).

13. See A. Kundnani, *The Muslims Are Coming! Islamophobia, Extremism and the Domestic War on Terror* (London/New York: Verso, 2014).

14. The co-chair of the Stop the Minarets Movement, SVP MP Ulrich Schlüer, was actually James Schwarzenbach's secretary in 1971.

3. Establishing Norms

1. Full text of speech available at conservative-speeches.sayit. mysociety.org.
2. Full citations for all the speeches by right politicians delivered throughout 2011 can be found in L. Fekete, 'Understanding the European-Wide Assault on Multiculturalism', in H. Mahamdallie, ed., *Defending Multiculturalism: A Guide for the Movement* (London: Bookmarks, 2012).
3. For an ongoing analysis of Orbán's racism, see *Hungarian Spectrum*, the daily blog of Eva S. Balogh, at hungarian spectrum.org.
4. As cited by E. Balogh. The full interview is available from *Bild*, 12 September 2015, at bild.de.
5. Samuel Huntington, *The Clash of Civilizations?*, Foreign Affairs, 72: 3 (1993).
6. Alain de Benoist, the founder of the Nouvelle Droite in France, sought to create a 'Gramscianism of the Right'. See R. van Kranenburg, 'Whose Gramsci? Right-Wing Gramscism', *International Gramsci Society Newsletter* 9 (March 1999). See also A. Mammone, 'The Transnational Reaction to 1968: Neo-Fascist Fronts and Political Cultures in France and Italy', *Contemporary European History* 17: 2 (2008).
7. For the UK, see M. Barker, *The New Racism: Conservatives and the Ideology of the Tribe* (London: Junction, 1981); P. Gordon and F. Klug, *New Right, New Racism* (London: Searchlight, 1986); N. Murray and C. Searle, *Racism and the Press in Thatcher's Britain* (London: Institute of Race Relations, 1989). For France, see T. Bar-On, *Rethinking the French New Right: Alternatives to Modernity* (London: Routledge, 2013); J. Wolfreys, 'An Iron Hand in a Velvet Glove: The Programme of the French Front National', *Parliamentary Affairs* 46: 3 (1993). For Germany, see R. Woods, *Germany's New*

Right as Culture and Politics (London: Palgrave Macmillan, 2007). For Italy, see Mammone, 'Transnational Reaction'.

8. Full text of speech available at theguardian.com.

9. See M. Carr, 'You Are Now Entering Eurabia', *Race & Class* 48: 1 (2006); L. Fekete, 'The Muslim Conspiracy Theory and the Oslo Massacre', *Race & Class* 53: 3 (2012).

10. See J. Müller, *A Dangerous Mind: Carl Schmitt in Post-War European Thought* (London: Yale University Press, 2003); Fritz Stern, *The Politics of Cultural Despair: A Study in the Rise of the Germanic Ideology* (Berkeley, CA: University of California Press, 1961).

11. N. MacMaster, *Racism in Europe: 1870–2000* (London: Palgrave Macmillan, 2001), p. 32.

12. See D. Luban, 'Carl Schmitt and the Critique of Lawfare', *Georgetown Public Law and Legal Theory Research Paper* 11–33 (2011).

13. See A. Kundnani, *The Muslims are Coming: Islamophobia, Extremism, and the Domestic War on Terror* (London: Verso, 2014), pp. 55–65.

14. For a critique see P. Hervik, 'Flemming Rose and the Absence of Empathy', IRR News Online, 26 February 2015, at irr.org.uk.

15. For a critique see A. Kundnani, *The End of Tolerance* (London: Pluto, 2007), pp. 87–9.

16. M. Meng, 'Silences about Sarrazin's Racism in Contemporary Germany', *Journal of Modern European History* 87 (2015).

17. 'The Man Who Divided Germany: Why Sarrazin's Integration Demagoguery Has Many Followers', Spiegel Online International, 6 September 2010, at spiegel.de.

18. A. Ryder, 'One Nation Conservatism: A Gypsy, Roma and Traveller case Study', *Race & Class* 57: 2 (2015).

19. J. Bourne, 'In Defence of Multiculturalism', IRR Briefing Paper 2, February 2007, at irr.org.uk.

20. J. Bourne, 'The Race Relations Act 1965: Blessing or Curse?' IRR News Online, 13 November 2015, at irr.org.uk

21. W. Baier, 'Europe at the Crossroads: Right Populism and Reactionary Rebellion', in L. Panitch and G. Albo, eds, *The Politics of the Right: Socialist Register 2016* (London: Merlin, 2015).

22. The words are those of then Labour home secretary David Blunkett, in his 'Integration with Diversity: Globalization and the Renewal of Democracy and Civil Society', Foreign Policy Centre (London, 2002).
23. A. Sivanandan, 'The Market State vs the Good Society', *Race & Class* 54: 3 (2013).
24. For a discussion of the social theory of nodal structures, see L. Weber, *Policing Non-Citizens* (Abingdon: Routledge, 2013), pp. 10–11.
25. See M. Mazower, *Governing the World: The History of an Idea* (London: Allen Lane, 2013), p. 420.
26. Baier, 'Europe at the Crossroads', p. 83.
27. R. Saul, 'Capitalism and the Politics of the Far Right', in Panitch and Albo, *Politics of the Far Right*, p. 144.

4. Xeno-Racism and the Making of 'Enemy Aliens'

1. For a moving account of the impact of deportation, see L. de Noronha, 'Two Flights: The Deportation Game', *Lacuna*, March 2016.
2. Although it is not the subject of this chapter, it should be pointed out that alongside the special prison regimes for foreign-national prisoners has grown up a special penal regime, in the Netherlands, Belgium, France, Spain and the UK, for Muslim terror suspects (both citizens and non-citizens). The special prison regimes being developed across Europe are 'prisons within prisons', characterised by excessive use of solitary confinement. For further information, see the website supermax.be.
3. Council of Europe, Annual Police Statistics, SPACE 1, 2015, updated 25 April 2017.
4. See S. Turnbull and I. Hasselberg, 'From Prison to Detention: The Carceral Trajectories of Foreign-National Prisoners in the UK', *Punishment and Society* 19: 2 (2016).
5. L. Dubinsky et al., 2012, Preface, xiii.
6. 'The Enemy on the Border: Critique of a Programme in Favour of a Preventative State', *Punishment and Society* 9: 3 (2007).

7. For a discussion of the work of both men, see E. Klein and C. Menke, *Der Mensch als Person und Rechtsperson: Die Grundlage der Freiheit* (Berlin: Berliner Wissenschafts-Verlag, 2011).

8. W. Weber, 'Leading German Newspaper's Conference Hears Call for Dismantling Democracy', World Socialist Web Site, 13 December 2012, at wsws.org.

9. J. Simon, *Governing through Crime* (Oxford: Oxford University Press, 2007).

10. The details of the case are set out in several articles in the 2013 graduation magazine of the German Journalists School, available as a pdf at djs-online.de.

11. See L. Fekete and M. Hoppe, 'Populist Anti-Asylum Movement Born at Kollum', *European Race Audit*, March 2000.

12. See, for example, J. Hooper, 'Italian Woman's Murder Prompts Expulsion Threat to Romanians', *Guardian*, 2 November 2007.

13. L. de Noronha, ' "Foreign Criminals" – Questioning the Consensus', Open Democracy, 30 October 2014, at open democracy.net.

14. As cited by Y. Musharbash, 'Vier Lehran aus der Silversternacht in Köln', *ZEITmagazin* ONLINE, 28 June 2016, at zeit.de.

15. M. Kötter, 'The (Not So) Slow Murder of the Geneva Convention', Transform Network blog, 22 January 2016, at transform-network.net.

16. Later reports, in fact, identified men from North African countries as the most common culprits.

17. For a feminist perspective, see the statement 'Against Sexualised Violence and Racism. Always. Anywhere. #ausmahmslos (#noexcuses)', at ausnahmslos.org. See also, 'From Egypt to Germany: Reflections about Sexual Violence from a Feminist Perspective in Light of the Cologne Attacks', Nazra for Feminist Studies, research paper, 8 March 2016, at nazra.org.

18. M. Ullgren, cited in 'European Media Face New Scrutiny of Reporting on Immigration and Crime,' *Christian Science Monitor*, 5 February 2016.

19. T. Meaney, 'Short Cuts', *London Review of Books*, 4 February 2016.

20. R. Andersson, 'Hunter and Prey: Patrolling Clandestine Migration in the Euro-African Borderlands', *Anthropological Quarterly* 87: 1 (2014).

21. See, Eugénie Bastié, 'Que Serait Devenu le Petit Aylan S'il Avait Grand?' *Charlie Hebdo* choque, *Le Figaro*, 14 January 2016.

22. See, for example, 'German Media Incites Racist Hysteria', World Socialist Web Site, 12 January 2016, at wsws.org.

5. The EU, Uneven Development and the Nationalist Backlash

1. M. Bénilde, 'The Creation of Emmanuel Macron', *Le Monde Diplomatique* (English edition), 7 May 2017, at mondediplo. com.

2. According to Perry Anderson, the EU is unquestionably a polity, but with two planes, national and supranational, and with an enormous structural gap between the institutions of Europe and its citizens. P. Anderson, *The New Old Order* (London: Verso, 2011), p. xi.

3. J. Meek, 'Somerdale to Skarbimierz', *London Review of Books*, 20 April 2017.

4. D. Stuckler, L. King and M. McKee, 'Mass Privatisation and the Post-Communist Mortality Crisis: A Cross-National Analysis', *Lancet* 53: 9,661 (2009).

5. P. Hamm, L. King and D. Stuckler, 'Mass Privatisation, State Capacity and Economic Growth in Post-Communist Countries', *American Sociological Review* 77: 2 (2012).

6. The Ervína Szabová Collective, 'Slovakia Needs an Alternative', *Jacobin*, 20 April 2016.

7. J. Cienski, 'New Media Law Gives Polish Government Fuller Control', *Politico*, 30 December 2015.

8. For Hungary, see N. Berend and C. Clark, 'Not Just a Phase', *London Review of Books*, 20 November 2014; E. Balogh, 'Orban's Veritas Institute Looks at Anti-Semitism in the Horthy Era', *Hungarian Spectrum*, 26 June 2016. For Poland,

see, for example, Alex Duval Smith, '"Vindictive" Polish Leaders Using New War Museum to Rewrite History, Says Academic', *Observer*, 24 April 2016.

9. See, for example, 'Hungary's Orban Criticizes Merkel's "Moral Imperialism"', *Deutsche Welle*, 23 September 2015.

10. B. Magyar, *The Post-Communist Mafia State: The Case of Hungary* (Budapest: Central European University Press, 2015).

11. See A. Nardelli, R. Mason and D. Pegg, 'Revealed: Tax Credit Data Exposes Limits of Cameron's "Emergency Break"', *Guardian*, 4 February 2016.

12. J. Müller, 'Angela Merkel's Misunderstood Christian Mission' (*Foreign Policy*, 18 March 2016) draws attention to the anti-Merkel cliques that were forming inside the EU, opposing Merkel's supposed 'relativism' and 'running after the Zeitgeist'.

13. F. Denord, R. Knaebel and P. Rimbert, 'Germany's Iron Cage', *Le Monde Diplomatique* (English edition), August 2015, at mondediplo.com.

14. See W. Streeck, 'Germany Can't Solve This Alone', *Le Monde Diplomatique* (English edition), May 2015, at mondediplo.com.

15. Anderson, *New Old World*, p. 26.

16. 'The Rise of the German Eurosceptic Party Alternative für Deutschland, between Ordoliberal Critique and Popular Anxiety', *International Political Science Review* 36: 3 (2016).

17 See T. Meaney, 'The New Star of Germany's Far Right', *New Yorker*, 3 October 2016.

18. Streeck, 'Germany Can't Solve This Alone'.

19. S. Kouvelakis, 'Syriza's Rise and Fall', *New Left Review* II/97 (January–February 2016).

20. See S. Halimi, 'The Europe We Don't Want', *Le Monde Diplomatique* (English edition), August 2015, at mondediplo.com; N. Kadritzke, 'Greece is Sold Off and Sold Out', *Le Monde Diplomatique* (English edition), July 2016, at mondediplo.com.

21. D. Howden and A. Fotiades, 'The Refugee Archipelago', *Guardian*, 9 March 2017.

22. Haris Golemis interviews Yanis Varoufakis, 'What Happened in Greece – What Was Possible – What Is a Feasible European-Wide Programme Now?', in *The Enigma of Europe* (Transform Network Yearbook) (London: Merlin, 2016).

23. The Madrid Metropolitan Observatory has analysed the impact of the financialisation of the housing market. See Isidro López and Emmanuel Rodríguez, 'The Spanish Model', *New Left Review* II/69 (May–June 2011).

24. N. Wonders, 'Transforming Borders from Below', in L. Weber, ed., *Rethinking Border Control for a Globalizing World: A Preferred Future* (London: Routledge, 2015).

25. H. Graham, 'The Sacred Dead', *London Review of Books*, 5 March 2015.

26. H. Graham, *The War and Its Shadow: Spain's Civil War in Europe's Long Twentieth Century* (Eastbourne: Sussex Academic Press, 2014), p. 151.

27. See R. Seymour, 'UKIP and the Crisis of Britain', in *The Politics of the Right: Socialist Register 2016* (London: Merlin, 2015).

28. See H. Astier, 'French National Front: Far Right or Hard Left?' BBC News, 16 May 2014.

29. Institute of Race Relations, *Racial Violence and the Brexit State* (London: IRR, 2016).

30. For a critique, see 'Fog in Channel, Historians Isolated: An Open Letter in Response to the Historians for Britain Campaign', *History Today*, 18 May 2015.

31. See R. Lefebvre, 'Socialist Party Falls Apart', *Le Monde Diplomatique* (English edition), July 2016, at mondediplo.com.

32. See P. Leymarie, 'No More Playing Policeman in Africa', *Le Monde Diplomatique* (English edition), April 2017, at mondediplo.com.

33. See M. F. Rech, 'Recruitment, Counter-Recruitment and Critical Military Studies', *Global Discourse* 4: 2–3 (2014).

34. M. Bostridge, 'Children Have No Place in the British Army', *Guardian*, 22 December 2015.

35. See C. Chadderton, 'The Militarisation of English Schools: Troops to Teaching and the Implications for Initial Teacher Education and Race Equality', *Race Ethnicity and Education* 17: 3 (2014).

36. See 'Gove Speech on "the Underclass" in Full', 1 September 2011, at politics.co.uk.
37. G. Agamben, 'For a Theory of Destituent Power', *Critical Legal Thinking*, 5 February 2014, at criticallegalthinking. com.
38. Ibid.
39. Ibid.
40. G. Viscusi, 'Terror Fight after Paris Attack Prompts Charge of Stifled Debate', Bloomberg, 3 February 2016, at bloomberg. com.
41. Amnesty International, *A Right Not a Threat: Disproportionate Restrictions on Demonstrations under the State of Emergency in France* (London: Amnesty International, 2017).
42. Prevention of Terrorism Act (2005); Terrorism Prevention and Investigation Measures Act (2011).
43. J. Gandini, 'Towards a Permanent State of Emergency,' *Le Monde Diplomatique* (English edition), January 2016, at mondediplo.com.

6. White Grievance and the Cult of Exit

1. For further discussion of GONGOs, see 'On "Shrinking Space": A Framing Paper', Amsterdam: Transnational Institute Briefing Paper, April 2017.
2. 'Strengthening the EU's Response to Radicalisation and Violent Extremism', European Commission, IP/14/18 15/01/2014.
3. 'Business is Booming for Sweden's Nazi Skinheads', *Searchlight*, January 1996. See also M. Deland, 'The Cultural Racism of Sweden', *Race & Class* 39: 1 (1997).
4. For a critical appraisal of Carlberg's views on 'positive nationalism', see Deland, 'Cultural Racism'.
5. For the history, see T. Bjørgo, 'Exit Neo-Nazism: Reducing Recruitment and Promoting Disengagement from Racist Groups', Norwegian Institute of International Affairs Paper No. 627 (June 2002).
6. See T. Bjørgo, 'How Gangs Fall Apart: Process of Transformation and Disintegration of Gangs', paper presented at the

Fifty-First Annual Meeting of the American Society of Criminology, Toronto, Canada, 18–20 November 1999.

7. Bjørgo, 'Exit Neo-Nazism', p. 9.

8. Ibid., p. 8.

9. Tor Bach, telephone interview (8 July 2014).

10. The Fryshuset also hosts the Centre for Information on Destructive Sub-Cultures (CIDES).

11. For an appraisal of Exit Motala and details of the split with Exit Stockholm, see C. Englund, 'Exit Motala: A Case Study', Expo Foundation, December 2012.

12. See 'We Provide the Way Out: De-Radicalization and Disengagement', revised second edition, Exit-Deutschland, 2014, available at file:///C:/Users/Liz/Downloads/Broschuere-EXIT-Engl_PDFDS_11.4%20(5).pdf.

13. Bjørgo, 'Exit Neo-Nazism'.

14. B. Klose, by email (16 June and 5 August 2014).

15. N. Greger, 'Verschenkte Jahre eine Jugend im Nazi-Hass', e-publication, booksondemand.com 2012. Another example within this genre is K. Lindhal, 'Exit: min väg bort från Nazismen' (Stockholm?: Norstedts, 2000).

16. M. Goodwin, 'Tommy Robinson's EDL Resignation was Disingenuous Nonsense', *Guardian*, 9 October 2013.

17. M. Townsend, 'British Far-Right Extremists Voice Support for Anders Breivik', *Observer*, 1 September 2012.

18. S.Aust and D. Laabs, *Heimatschutz: Der Statt und die Mordserie des NSU* (Munich: Pantheon, 2012).

19. See Committee on the Administration of Justice, *Covert Policing and Ensuring Accountability: Ten Years On from the Cory Collusion Inquiry Reports, Where Now?* (Belfast: CAJ, 2016).

20. Ibid.

21. A. von der Behrens (the lawyer representing the family of Mehmet Kubaşık, murdered by the NSU in April 2006), police informers, by email (8 July 2014).

22. Deland, 'Cultural Racism', p. 57.

23. For an earlier critique of white victimhood frameworks, see L. Fekete, 'Let Them Eat Cake', *Race & Class* 39: 3 (1998).

24. For a critique, see K. Engelhart, 'How to "Cure" a Nazi', VICE Online, 18 February 2014, at vice.com.

25. The quotes are taken from two separate reports by the Institute for Strategic Dialogue that can be downloaded from its website: 'The Role of Civil Society in Counter Radicalisation and De-Radicalisation' and 'Review of Programs to Counter Narratives of Vilent Extremism'.

26. J. Pilger, 'Understanding the Latest Prism Leaks Is Understanding the Rise of a New Fascism', *New Statesman*, 20 June 2013.

7. The Market in Asylum and the Outsourcing of Force

1. A. Gordon, by email (26 August 2016).

2. J. Darling, 'Privatising Asylum: Neoliberalisation, Depoliticisation and the Governance of Forced Migration', Transactions of the Institute of British Geographers, 2016.

3. J. Ferguson and A. Gupta, 'Spatialising States: Towards an Ethnography of Neoliberal Governmentality', *American Ethnologist* 29 (2002).

4. See F. Stonor Saunders, 'Where on Earth Are You?', *London Review of Books*, 3 March 2016.

5. P. Andreas, 'Redrawing the Line: Borders and Security in the Twenty-First Century', *International Security* 78: 2 (2003).

6. Ibid., p. 79.

7. Corporate Watch, *Snitches, Stings and Leaks: How 'Immigration Enforcement' Works* (London: CW, 2016).

8. 'African Civil Society Condemns the Hunt for Migrants on the Continent', Statewatch, May 2016, at statewatch.org.

9. E. S. Balogh, '"Border Hunters" Join Soldiers and Policemen at the Serbian–Hungarian Border', *Hungarian Spectrum*, 25 August 2016, at hungarianspectrum.org.

10. J. Brachet, 'Policing the Desert: The IOM in Libya Beyond War and Peace', *Antipode* 48: 2 (2016).

11. See F. Webber, 'Europe's Unknown War', *Race & Class* 59: 1 (2017).

12. See L. Lewis Smith and M. Umunna, 'A Special Gift from UK to Nigeria: Promoting Human Rights or Secrecy?' Open Democracy, 20 September 2016, at opendemocracy.net.

13. R. Andersson, 'Hunter and Prey: Patrolling Clandestine

Migration in the Euro-African Borderlands', *Anthropological Quarterly* 87: 1 (2014).

14. See 'More Neighbours Makes More Fences', *Economist*, 7 January 2016.

15. See D. Howden, 'How the Private Sector Can Help Tackle the Refugee Crisis', Refugees Deeply, 3 October 2016, at newsdeeply.com; E. Morozov, 'Beware the "Empathy-Washing" of Self-Proclaimed Caring Capitalists', *Observer*, 2 July 2016.

16. L. Arbogast, 'Migrant Detention in the European Union: A Thriving Business' (Brussels: Migreurop and Rosa Luxemburg Stiftung, June 2016), at migreurop.org, p. 54.

17. L. Weber and S. Pickering, *Globalization and Borders: Death at the Global Frontier* (London: Palgrave Macmillan, 2011).

18. Migszol, 'The Catastrophic Consequences of the 8km Law and Violence at the Hungarian–Serbian Border', 6 August 2016, at migszol.com; Human Rights Watch, 'Hungary: Migrants Abused at the Border', 13 July 2016, at hrw.org.

19. M. Townsend, 'Protests Grow as Greece Moves Refugees to Warehouses "Not Fit for Animals" ', *Guardian*, 28 May 2016.

20. The Nauru files comprise more than 2,000 incident reports leaked from inside Australia's asylum seeker detention regime, covering assaults, sexual abuse, self-harm attempts, child abuse and living conditions. The *Guardian* has created a unique database where all the documents are stored.

21. B. O'Brien and R. Ball, *Association with Abuse: The Financial Sector's Association with Gross Human Rights Abuses of People Seeking Asylum in Australia* (Melbourne: GetUP and Human Rights Law Centre, 2016).

22. See Liberty, *G4S: A History of Discrimination, Human Rights Violations, Malpractice and Mismanagement in the UK* (London: Liberty, 2016).

23. See, in particular, John Grayson, 'G4S Asylum Housing Fiasco Descends into Farce', Open Democracy, 15 May 2013, at opendemocracy.net; and 'Bed Bugs and Freight Sheds: Britain's Welcome to Asylum Seekers', Open Democracy, 6 April 2016, at opendemocracy.net.

24. Grayson, 'Bed Bugs and Freight Sheds'.

25. See A. Berger, 'Flüchtlings-Lager in Calden: Mitarbeiter

kritisieren Vorgesetzte und Situation', HNA, 17 February 2016; G. Henke, 'Ex-Mitarbeiter des Caldener Flüchtlingslagers verklagt Wachfirma', HNA, 27 April 2016.

26. B. Kadletz, 'Abandonment and Violence in Calais', Refugees Deeply, 7 September 2016, at newsdeeply.com.
27. Cited in C. Fouteau, 'Calais and Grande-Synthe: A Tale of Two Radically Different Migrant Camps', Mediapart, 15 March 2016, at mediapart.fr.
28. 'Design and Racism', *Funambulist* (special issue), May–June 2016, at thefunambulist.net.
29. See La Parisienne Liberee, 'The Shameful Container Camp for Calais Migrants', 22 January 2016, at mediapart.fr.

8. 'They Shall Not Pass'

1. In July 2015, five Spanish migrant workers of Gambian and Senegalese origin were crushed to death after a concrete wall collapsed at Hawkeswood Metal recycling centre, near Birmingham, where there had been two previous serious safety incidents in recent years.
2. See A. Chakrabortty, 'How Boots Went Rogue' *Guardian*, 13 April 2016; S. Goodley and J. Ashby, 'A Day at "the Gulag": What It's Like to Work at Sports Direct's Warehouse', *Guardian*, 9 December 2015; F. Lawrence, 'This Is a Brutal and Inhumane Way to Treat Staff – and Sports Direct is Not Alone', *Guardian*, 8 June 2016.
3. See F. Lawrence, 'Poultry Workers Win Compensation in High Court for Slavery', *Guardian*, 10 June 2016.
4. See A. Sivanandan, 'The Market State vs the Good Society', *Race and Class* 54: 3 (2013).
5. Ibid.
6. See C. Douzinas, H. Kouki and A. Vradis, 'The Arrest of Golden Dawn's Leader Will Do Little to Counter Institutional Racism', *Guardian*, 29 September 2013.
7. L. Weber and S. Pickering, *Globalization and Borders: Death at the Global Frontier* (Melbourne: Palgrave Macmillan, 2011), pp. 51–6.

8. For Hannah Arendt, the problem of truth presented itself to Walter Benjamin as a 'revelation ... that must be heard, that is, which lies in the metaphysically acoustical sphere'. See her introduction to W. Benjamin, *Illuminations* (London: Pimlico, 1999), p. 53.

Index

Index